More Praise for
The Woman's Book of Spirit

"If you loved *Simple Abundance*, you will savor this book. These beautiful and wise meditations help us all nurture and live from our hearts. Only then can we turn outward to replenish the world's wellspring with much needed compassion, tolerance, and love."
—Susan Skog, author of *Embracing Our Essence: Spiritual Conversations with Prominent Women*

"With a finely tuned heart and the power of well-crafted words, Sue Patton Thoele opens a door to the often hidden treasures of the sacred. Treasures which impregnate the nitty-gritty of a woman's life."
—Paula Payne Hardin, author of *Love after Love* and *What are You Doing for the Rest of Your Life?*

"Sue Patton Thoele's books have been part of my daily spiritual practice for years. Reading The Woman's Book of Spirit provides a generous portion of spiritual nourishment to everyday life. The passages are offered with great respect and loving kindness from a wise and experienced traveler on the spiritual journey."
—Vimala McClure, author of *The Tao of Motherhood* and *A Woman's Guide to Tantra Yoga*

Other Books in the Series

The Woman's Book of Courage
The Woman's Book of Confidence

The Woman's Book *of* Spirit

The Woman's Book *of* Spirit

. . . .

MEDITATIONS FOR
THE THIRSTY SOUL

. . . .

SUE PATTON THOELE

CONARI PRESS
Berkeley, CA

Conari Press books are distributed by
Publishers Group West

Cover Design: Leigh Wells
Cover illustration: Rae Ecklund
Author photo: Paige Eden Thoele

ISBN: 1-57324-056-7

Library of Congress Cataloging-in-Publication Data
Thoele, Sue Patton.
    The woman's book of spirit: meditations for the thirsty
soul / Sue Patton Thoele.
        p. cm.
    ISBN 1-57324-056-7 (trade paper: alk. paper)
    1. Women—Religious life.   2. Meditations.   I. Title.
BL625.7.T46   1997
291.4'32'082—dc21   97–3912

Printed in the United States of America
on recycled paper.

10 9 8 7 6 5 4 3 2 1

So vast is the nature of spirit that the energies which flow into it can never fill it, nor those which flow from it exhaust it.

Dedication

....

To my beloved and beautiful mother, Virginia, who loved me well in life and loves me still after death. "Mother, your questing soul inspired my spiritual exploration. Thank you!"

With unending gratitude to my spiritual mother, Annabelle, whose wisdom, light, and love have guided me from my very first spiritual baby-steps.

Contents

....

3. Nourishing Our Souls, 66

Gathering at the Well

I am so excited to be writing *The Woman's Book of Spirit*. It's a blessing to be given the opportunity to talk about what a majority of us know in the dark and fertile depths of our hearts, but sometimes lose sight of during the glare and whirl of everyday life. And that is: Women are spiritually endowed. This is not to say that men aren't also spiritually gifted, but we women seem to intuitively know how to live from our hearts where the essence of our Spirit resides. From our hearts spring what I refer to as the Sacred Feminine Voice.

To be sure, over the last several hundred years, attempts have been made by society, both consciously and unconsciously, to freeze-dry the feminine voice and spirit, stuff it in a corked jar, and store it on a musty shelf somewhere in a remote and shadowy closet. The attempts certainly were successful on me. For many years as my own sense of spirit seemed to lay dormant, I felt no sense of connection to either a divine being or to the divinity within myself. Although I did what I was raised to do—go to church, have a nice family, be a nice person—underneath it all ran a vague river of discontent and a profound thirst for a sense of an intimate and joyful relationship with God and my own spirit.

The universe has a magical way of responding to our deep longings and it answered mine with a swift kick in the teeth. My husband fell in love with my best friend and left me. I was reduced to a blithering, emotional puddle and could do very little else but stagger into the arms of God and crawl, bleeding, onto a spiritual path. Turns out it was the biggest favor anyone has ever done for me.

Out of that trauma, I eventually became aware that spirituality is simple. Fundamentally, we are spiritual beings with soul as our essence, our most basic quality. We've forgotten. I continue to forget on a daily basis. Consequently, it seems to me that a huge spiritual lesson for most of us is to re-remember, to re-evolve into simplicity of spirit, and invite the natural, inherent essence of our Selves back to the fore of our lives, to "become like little children."

I believe women are being called to birth this all important spirit-memory. In order for our relationships, our lives, and perhaps our very planet to thrive, we must free our spiritual essence from its relegated closet. Only then can love flow continually into our hearts from the Divine and overflow onto others. Women are inherently vessels of love, and through our love and spiritual connection, we can rescue the parched and perishing within and among us.

Countless women are doing this right now. Through tears, rituals, honoring, acknowledging, and learning from each other, we are healing our wounds and opening our hearts. We are remembering and connecting with our own inherent spiritual core and with the core of others. Rising from the ashes of injustice, domination, and fear, we women are reclaiming our heritage as essentially spiritual beings who are learning and growing through human experience. Since you are reading these words, I have no doubt that you're already dipping your chalice into the well of soul, or, if not, that you are intensely aware of your yearning and desire to do so.

Before *The Woman's Book of Spirit* was even a seed of an idea, the Sacred Feminine Voice whispered in my ear regarding the writing of it. Having just finished *Heart Centered Marriage*, I was in a typical let-down mood, a creative lull that often follows a period of intense work. Not being overly crazy about the feeling, I decided to ask during meditation what my purpose and goals were now that my current project was completed. I am not a wildly psychic person who regularly receives a lot of "phenomena" but, during this meditation, unexplained yet very clear, a message was delivered: *Pour water upon my women.*

Because I was already deeply committed to reclaiming the Sacred Feminine Voice in myself, relationships, and the world in general, I felt the message pertained to revitalizing and reintroducing feminine values. But there seemed to be more that I wasn't understanding. I asked to be shown the significance of the enigmatic message. It wasn't until Brenda, one of the wonderful women at Conari Press, said to me, "Why don't you write a third meditation book entitled *The Woman's Book of Spirit?*" that the message became clear. A resounding "Yes!" careened through my heart and mind, and I fell deeply and passionately in love with the idea of writing about women's thirst for soul.

Although I was immediately riding the crest of a wave toward the creation of this book as soon as the idea was mentioned, by no means do I think I have the answer, or any answers for that matter. To me, *Pour water upon my women* was an invitation to share with you some of my own, my friends', and my clients' experiences along our very different spiritual paths: to pour the water of our spirits out for you to drink in, relate to, and take comfort in. If our stories are helpful in moistening and revitalizing your heart and creating more balance and harmony in your inner and outer lives, then I will be thrilled.

The Woman's Book of Spirit can be used in a number of ways—as a meditation guide, a daily friend, or the answer to a specific question. You may want to use it as a powerful intuitive exercise by opening it at random after holding it to your heart and asking your inner wisdom to guide you to the perfect, right entry for you at this moment.

Our hearts are the seat of the soul, holding within them the marvelous and mysterious power that spiritual seekers have pondered for ages. Interestingly, the power of the heart is now being measured in scientific laboratories. Recently, I attended a seminar at the Institute of HeartMath in Boulder Creek, California. The Institute's studies are providing compelling evidence that activating heart energy harmonizes the body/mind connection, reduces stress, and increases well-being physically, emotionally, mentally, and spiritually. The best news of all is that each of us can choose to activate these healing and reviving heart frequencies. It is my hope that these meditations will help you do just that.

This is a very exciting time in human history. Women everywhere are gathering at the spring-fed wells of our beings to pour the water of our spirits on each other, to share our hearts, to join hands as we move toward more completely expressing our boundless love, magnificent wisdom, and compassionate intuition. To these limitless wells, each of us carries her own container. Each of us fills her own jar. And, each of us is also called to walk with her sisters along the way providing support, guidance, encouragement, inspiration, and love. All of us, men and women alike, are asked to birth a more soulful way of being, to create a more spiritually harmonious way to live, and to open our hearts in order to spread love, compassion, care, and healing.

Re-Greening
Arid Places

It's essential that we understand that taking care of the planet will be done as we take care of ourselves. You know that you can't really make much of a difference in things until you change yourself.

—Alice Walker

THE GREAT ELEVENTH-CENTURY CHRISTIAN mystic, scholar, and physician, Hildegaard of Bingen, defined sin as spiritual dry-rot, aridity, and refusal to grow. She believed that the opposite of sin was to be gloriously and outrageously alive—green and moist, like nature. Water, a common metaphor for both spirit and femininity, is our most obvious greening agent. In order to grow into the beautiful women we were created to be, we must pour the waters of spirit upon our arid places.

All of us have draught-ridden areas within us that need watering and reclamation. The wonderful news is that even a desert wasteland can be turned into a lush oasis when irrigated with enough water and planted with the right seeds. The same is true of us. No matter how dry or barren some aspects of ourselves or our lives may feel, they can be reclaimed when sanctified by the powerful feminine waters of compassion, forgiveness, right thought, acceptance, and gentle guidance.

Paying Attention to Your Soul's Garden

....

PLANTS ARE WONDERFUL SPIRITUAL TEACHERS. When we pay attention to their simple needs, they respond by growing and bringing beauty and life-giving oxygen into our presence. Plants silently make us aware of their needs by wilting, yellowing, or failing to thrive. Equally silent, but often less obvious, our soul-needs can go unnoticed for long periods of time. If the needs of our spiritual self are ignored too long, drought conditions occur, leaving us feeling dried up and lifeless.

Luckily, both flowers and spirits are very resilient and respond beautifully to a little nurturance. Recently, I was all wrapped up in my work and totally forgot that my potted geraniums and impatiens were sweltering in a heat wave. By the time I noticed them, the impatiens were already crispy. Plying them with fervent apologies and much needed water, I urged them to revive. Miraculously, they did. Given a little attention and tender loving care, our spirits are just as forgiving and equally as anxious to re-green and bloom as were my flowers.

What does your soul garden look like? Are the plants and flowers green and happy? If not, what will quench their thirst? What attention do they crave? What tiny little step can you take right now? What miniature bloom can you attend to soon?

When you listen attentively, you'll know how best to serve your soul's needs. It's very important, however, that we don't try to do too much at once or we set ourselves up for failure and become discouraged. When we consistently sow one small seed, water a single vase, till a square inch of soil, the entire garden reaps the benefit. Taking little soul-seconds—one small prayer, a few-minute meditation, a short burst of gratitude while appreciating nature—helps immeasurably to revive our thirsty spirits.

We don't have to join a convent or live in a cave to attend to our souls, although I admit that it sounds appealing sometimes. Luckily, our souls flower and grow when nurtured with consistent rays of attention interspersed among the busy hours of our days.

I pay attention to the needs of my spirit.
I make time to quench my soul's thirst.

Loving Self to Life

AS WOMEN, WE'RE OFTEN TRAINED TO LOVE others a lot, and ourselves a little. Unfortunately this is a backward concept because we're better able to love others when we first love ourselves. I know this idea has been harped on, but that's because it is absolutely true and truth deserves a little harp serenade. Just because the idea of self-love is widely accepted doesn't mean it's easy to do. But no matter how hard it may be for us to practice, it is essential, because lack of self-love and acceptance is the basis for most emotional problems, including the feelings of lifelessness and depression that plague so many women.

Fundamentally, loving ourselves is the best way to re-green our lives into the luxurious and creative lushness that we deserve. Unfortunately, there is no quick-fix, easy answer as to how to do this. Some of us were lucky enough to be taught to love ourselves when we were kids, but, for the rest of us, commitment to loving ourselves and a hundred daily decisions to "take ourselves to heart" are the only ways I've found that work. And they are by no means instantaneous. That's why I firmly believe that becoming consistently and compassionately self-loving is one of our lifelong spiritual tasks.

It seems easiest for most women to begin the self-loving process by loving their younger selves first. Picturing the little girls we were at about three years old and then showering them with the love that they needed and deserved is a great place to start. If you can't bring yourself to love this little one, call in a marvelously maternal and loving being to cherish and cuddle her for you. When I feel especially needy, I hug a large teddy bear and pretend that it's the "little Susie" inside me who feels unloved or unlovable.

Since love is the only energy that brings lasting change, our sacred charge is to love ourselves to life.

I am loveable.

Each day it becomes easier for me to love myself.

Keeping Anger Moist
and Movable

ANGER IS AN OUT-OF-HEART EXPERIENCE. That doesn't mean that it's a terrible no-no and that we shouldn't feel it or express it.

In fact, examined anger is often an incredible teacher. Exploring our experience of anger non-judgmentally often helps us uncover valuable clues as to what we expect, what we want, what we fear, and where we feel especially vulnerable. Indeed, examined anger is a spiritual ally. Examined anger remains moist and movable, supple and malleable to our inquiring minds. From it, we can learn to stop accepting the unacceptable in terms of treatment directed toward us.

However, unexamined and consequently suppressed or repressed anger is a different story. Very often it solidifies into resentment which shuts down our hearts and leeches all joy from our lives. In effect, resentment holds a gun to our heart and says, "Beware! You better dry up, and protect yourself. Opening up is dangerous." Resentment almost always guarantees aridity.

I don't know about you, but I was vigorously trained in anger-aversion and was an apt student. One of my primary life lessons continues to be transforming my self-loathing and self-judgment whenever I feel anger, and learning to use it constructively.

One great way I've found to keep anger moist and movable is to take it less seriously. Anger is great fodder for humor, and when expressed as such, we're often able to lighten up and laugh. For example, after an incredibly unfair divorce settlement, a friend of ours had Gene and I doubled over with laughter as he expounded dramatically about the book he was going to write: *How to Hold onto Your Anger when It's All You've Got Left!* Through humor, he was healthfully expressing just how upset he was at the injustice of his divorce. His intention was to learn from and move through his anger, but for now, it was giving him the energy he needed to walk this piece of the road.

Give yourself permission to explore and express your anger lightly and from the heart. As the saying goes, "What does it matter if a teaspoon of vinegar is spilled on a hill of sugar?"

I take my anger lightly.

I examine my anger and learn from it.

De-Idealizing Expectations

. . . .

A WOMAN I ADMIRE ONCE COMPLIMENTED me by saying, "Nowhere in your books did I find a shred of judgment." Luckily, my books are edited, but unfortunately my life is not. Judgment is an ongoing issue for me and for most of my clients.

Judgment arises when our expectations are not met, but often our expectations are idealized and unattainable and, therefore, impossible to meet. When I have gone deeply into examining my tendency to judge, I've found at the root, a set of impossible standards that I hold myself to, which inhibit my ability to love myself and others. Self-judgment gives rise to judgment of others—and both suck the love-enhancing moisture right out of our hearts and create draught conditions in our relationships.

Jamie was going through a very rough period in her marriage and was judging herself harshly for not being able to remain a calm and totally loving parent at all times. From my point of view, she was doing a great job under difficult circumstances. Her husband was in the military and virtually never home, her own emotions were in an uproar, and her sense of security in their future together was teetering precariously. Then, one day, a friend commented to her, "To love perfection is to hate life," which affected Jamie deeply. This profound little sentence helped her understand, at a gut level, what a burden she was placing on herself by expecting perfection in a far from perfect situation.

Although it was not easy for her, Jamie sought therapy and began learning the skills for de-idealizing her expectations and concentrating on self-acceptance rather than self-judgment. Over time the results of her work led to a greater tolerance of her imperfections, an increased ability to flow with life, more relaxed kids, and a revitalized marriage.

As human beings, we are evolving, maturing, and changing continually. It is unrealistic and discouraging to expect perfection from ourselves or others. Letting go of unrealistic ideals frees us to love more and, ironically enough, allows us to be better people.

I love life, imperfections and all.
I love myself, imperfections and all.

Fostering Self-Forgiveness

. . . .

ONE OF THE MOST EFFECTIVE WAYS TO BLEED our spirit-energy away is to impale ourselves on the twin swords of blame and nonforgiveness. Therefore, the ability to forgive ourselves is essential to our soul's growth. Forgiveness originally meant "to return good treatment for ill usage," which reminds me of a beautiful saying: "Forgiveness is the fragrance the violet sheds on the hand that has crushed it."

We are all susceptible to human failings. We've all pointed the finger of blame at ourselves and others and trotted out an inner perfectionist to bludgeon ourselves with guilt and shame. We have crushed the delicate violet of another's feelings and trampled our own under the heels of unrealistic demands. But as the imminently true cliche states, "To err is human, to forgive, divine." As we forgive, the divine fragrance of the Beloved flows through us, bestowing blessings.

Our souls are no strangers to forgiveness, for they have basked in the benediction of God's forgiveness for eternity. Difficulty in forgiving means that we have slipped from the heart of God into our human heads or guts and are no longer centered in the ground of our being, which is unconditional love.

By becoming aware of the skid away from our higher self, we can move back into our hearts. Even though it may sound too good to be true, we *can* return to our heart by merely asking to do so and accepting that it is done. Remembering to pour the fragrance of God's love and acceptance upon ourselves will set the stage for our ability to forgive the hands that occasionally crush us.

Forgiving ourselves allows us to create a garden of violets that will perfume our own and other's lives with the fragrance of love.

I am willing to forgive myself.

I forgive myself.

Extending Forgiveness

FORGIVENESS IS NOT OPTIONAL IF YOU WISH to walk a spiritual path. Practicing the art of forgiveness is essential for keeping our spirits green and gloriously alive. Not being able or willing to forgive those who have hurt us blocks God's love from entering our hearts and dams the flow of love going from us toward others.

Not forgiving binds us to our tormentor and to the original injury, keeping it fresh and current even if it is actually old and stale. Definitely a losing proposition! In reality, we don't forgive someone because it is good for the other person; we forgive in order to free our own hearts and souls and return ourselves to a state of love.

Tiffany was finding it very difficult to forgive her mother who drank herself to death when Tiffany was a teenager. The years preceding her mother's death were filled with neglect and embarrassment that had left deep scars. Grieving the fact that she had never really had a mother and venting her anger about her loss was important in Tiffany's healing. But eventually she realized that she didn't want to carry the ghost of her mother on her back for the rest of her life, and so she made a commitment to forgiving her.

Tiffany found it very helpful to picture her mother and then imagine that she could look *through* the drinker's facade and see the wounded, scared, and ignorant part of her mother who needed to disrupt everyone's lives. It was much easier to forgive the little girl inside her mother, who had also had a difficult childhood, than it was to forgive the woman who had made Tiffany's miserable.

In any forgiveness practice, it's important to remember that we can't see the whole spiritual picture. We don't know precisely what lessons our souls have signed up for in their evolutionary process. What we do know is that being able to forgive ourselves and others opens our hearts to the flow of divine energy.

I am willing to forgive _____.

I forgive _____.

Exploring the Family Tree

. . . .

IF WE HAVE ARID PLACES IN US FROM OUR experience with our parents, a great way to re-green them is to learn to understand, honor, and know our parents as human beings, not roles. If they are alive, we can talk to them about their childhoods and, by listening to their reminiscences, get a better feel for why and how they became the people they are. If our parents have died, we can talk to other family members and friends about them and explore letters and papers left behind.

Out of a deep desire to know who her father really was, Carrie created a four-page question-naire and sent it to him. It had easy questions like, "What is your favorite color?" and "What were your parents like?" and tough ones such as, "How did you want me to think or feel about my sexuality?" and "Do you think about your own death, and are you afraid?" Although it took him a while to respond, to his credit, this quiet man attempted to answer most of his daughter's questions.

Carrie told me that his answers gave her a feeling of comfort and calm, an increased sense of why she is who she is, and a richer picture of her background. She better understands the influences that shaped both herself and her father, and she feels closer to him as a result.

In knowing our parents, we can more fully know ourselves. Ask yourself how you might be able to know your parents more authentically and decide what actions you want to take that are appropriate to your circumstances. Doing so may feel like a risk, but, who knows—within their histories, you may find an oasis for yourself.

Our personalities yearn to know and understand our souls. And when either is revealed, the other becomes more transparent, more readily available.

I love to learn about my background.
I love and honor myself and my parents.

Trailing Clouds of Glory

GENE AND I RECENTLY BECAME GRANDPARENTS for the first time, and I am learning that nothing re-greens the heart and mind quite like being in the presence of an innocent infant. William Wordsworth was certainly right in his poem *Ode on Immortality* when he said, "But trailing clouds of glory do we come from God, who is our home: Heaven lies about us in our infancy!"

I've always gone to pet stores or stopped people on the street with infants, puppies, or kittens to get my baby-fixes, but the other day I stepped back just a little to view other family members reacting to my little grandbaby's first smiles. We had all turned into "people-puddles," melting in the warmth of the absolutely pure energy he embodies and showers on us. It's a two-way street—he opens our hearts with the aura of Heaven he trails, and we enfold him in love and security.

Not only can we make sure that we get a baby-fix every now and then, but we can re-green arid places within us by giving to and gleaning from our own inner little ones.

Pam's mother died only a few days after she

was born and Pam was cared for by a well-meaning but unprepared aunt who, not unnaturally, was a bit resentful at the unexpected turn of events in her life. As an adult, Pam avoided intimate relationships, rationalizing that she was too busy with her career. In truth, being a motherless daughter had left her carrying the unconscious belief that she was unlovable.

Finally, chronic depression made her seek therapy, where she discovered she needed to become the mother to herself that she'd never had. Through guided meditation, journaling, and a dogged determination to feel better, Pam began to love her inner infant and ultimately came to twin realizations: that she was not responsible for her mother's death and that she was infinitely lovable.

If you're feeling somewhat barren or lifeless, treat yourself to a baby-fix—either inner or outer—and immerse yourself in the innocent Heaven of new life.

I allow new life of all kinds to renew me.

I love my own inner little one.

Accepting Love from the Beloved

ONE OF THE BEST WAYS TO RE-GREEN ARID places in our psyches is to cultivate the skill of accepting and absorbing love. What is more nurturing than resting in the tender embrace of a loved one? What revitalizes us as much as feeling gently and unconditionally accepted? Very little, and yet it is often hard for us to both accept love and to ask for it. As with any skill, however, we can learn how to do it.

Gayle, a client of mine, was going through a very painful divorce. As a result, she felt betrayed, enraged, terrified, and totally unlovable. Although her friends and family tried to love and support her, she found it almost impossible to accept what they, or I, offered. As we worked together and her anger and terror dissipated somewhat, Gayle realized that the "plexiglass dome" she'd erected around herself was only serving to alienate her kids and make everyone, including herself, increasingly miserable. In a wonderfully passionate manner, Gayle decided that the best way to "get even with the bad guy" was to be happy.

Knowing that the ability to accept love was a big step toward happiness, Gayle committed herself to mastering the skill. She began each morning by telling her reflection in the mirror, "I love you" or, on really hard days, "I'm, sort of, a little willing to love you." A very determined woman, each day Gayle visualized herself being in the presence of a loving and caring spiritual being, and she practiced consciously accepting love from her. At first the exercise was very hard and felt phony, but she persevered. Next she practiced laying her hands on her heart and asking it to open when her children offered her love or she wanted to show love to them.

Although it took quite a while for Gayle to heal her hurt and learn to once more embrace love, today she is a happy woman with a close relationship to God, herself, and her family.

You, too, can become adept at welcoming love. Make a commitment today to be open to accepting love, and visualize being held in a loving embrace by the Great Spirit.

God is the Beloved who kisses me on the inside of my heart.

I am worthy of love.

Balancing God's Qualities

. . . .

I'VE HEARD IT SAID THAT IF GOD IS MALE, then the male is God, and in our predominately patriarchal culture, God's masculinity does remain the prevalent belief system. But in this belief something crucial to us all has been left out—the Feminine. Indeed the loss of the Feminine from our spiritual ideologies has caused a grief so deep and so raw, particularly in women, that it has been virtually unspeakable until recently. Why? Because, as women, we have been disinherited; we are not created in His image. In her book, *A God Who Looks Like Me*, Patricia Reilly beautifully addresses the wounding some women feel around this issue.

But the loss is not women's alone. No matter how we may feel about the idea of a purely male God, it is obvious that when the Divine is only masculine, only male qualities are highly valued. This leaves the feminine qualities of compassion, inclusion, cooperation, tolerance, beingness, intuition, and nurturance underrated and even perceived as weak or ineffective. With the negation of heart-qualities such as these comes many of the malignancies in society; lack of empathy, elevation of power, violence, disregard for nature, concentration solely on the mind to the exclusion of the heart, and loss of soul, to name only a few.

In a human family, it is optimal when both loving masculine and feminine models are available. The same is true within our spiritual family. Believing in and honoring both the masculine and feminine divinity within our hearts, and within the great unknowable mystery that is God, is essential for the balance and harmony of our spirits.

We need both the law and the love, the word and the wisdom, the mind and the heart of God. With tender honesty, ask yourself if the God that you love possesses both feminine and masculine aspects. If not, make a commitment to give yourself a sacred gift by incorporating the missing virtues into your heart's vision of the Beloved.

I honor and appreciate both the masculine and the feminine qualities of the Divine.

I possess qualities worthy of honor and admiration.

Finding the Motherhood of God

. . . .

ALTHOUGH I BELIEVE THAT GOD IS BIGGER than I can ever hope to fathom and embodies both masculine and feminine qualities, I often feel a deep yearning to sit at the feet of an ideal Mother God to be consoled or taught.

It wasn't until my own mother's last illness that I became fully aware of how much I longed for an unconditionally loving female presence. I wanted, both within me and in my spiritual ideology, a guide and plumb line who represented the feminine principles of love, wisdom, and patience. Jolted by the recognition that my most important female influence would soon be unavailable in physical form, I began to pray for and meditate on a feminine aspect of God to whom I could relate.

God responded to my request in beautiful ways. Teachers appeared as I was ready, and the two most important things I learned from them were very simple: *Your desire is valid and essential* and *Trust your images.*

As I began to trust my own images, they became clearer and more frequent. Right now, I'm aware of several female beings who comfort and guide me. One in particular, whom I call "The

Lady," appeared as a result of a knocked-to-my-knees, end-of-my-rope plea. She is incredibly strong, about seven feet tall, infinitely wise, and impersonally compassionate.

Please understand that I realize that I haven't a clue as to the reality of the mystery of God. The best I can do is love, honor, and serve the images that resonate with my heart at this time. But frankly, I don't think God cares what we call Him/Her/All, as long as we keep in touch.

I trust my images of God.

I ask for the Mother God who is right for me.

Walking the Earth
with Sensitive Feet

. . . .

IN A PERPETUAL DANCE, EARTH AND SKY provide us with a beautiful life-sustaining environment. Just when Mother Earth pulls back into her roots to replenish and revitalize, leaving her queendom brown and barren, Father Sky fills his realm with a carnival of clouds that bring moisture to a parched planet. Working in concert, they never leave us with a time when our eyes cannot be dazzled, our hearts uplifted in awe, and our lungs filled with air. Regretfully, ignorance and greed are damaging both earth and sky as we humans act as if there is an extra earth in the attic.

One outcome of living more in harmony with the Spirit will be a natural increase in awareness about the need to care for our planet. It is the literal ground of our being, and both Mother Earth and Father Sky need us to be sensitive to what harms them. We are planetary stewards and must learn to treat our home with respect and care.

Every now and then I travel to sacred spots with a group of spiritually-minded women. Recently we went to Arches National Park in Moab, Utah, where Mother Nature has responded to the elements of wind and water by creating breathtaking sculptures, awesome in size and beauty. One of the goals of these excursions is to consciously bless the earth and restore energy to places that may have been depleted through misuse.

On this trip, we spent two hours silently in the presence of the incredible arches. The single suggestion made by one of the leaders before we began was to hold the sentiment, "I see you from afar, and I am longing for your healing" as we experienced Mother Earth. Afterward, one woman's comment especially struck me: "I promised that I will walk the earth with sensitive feet."

How different our world would be if we all walked everywhere with sensitive feet! Take a moment today to consider your relationship with nature. How can you walk the earth with more sensitive feet?

I appreciate and care for the planet.

I see you from afar, and I am longing for your healing.

Learning from the Stones

GLEANING WISDOM FROM INDIGENOUS AND Eastern cultures who revere their elders, our heretofore youth-worshiping society is finally learning to let go of "age anxiety" and value the patina that aging can bring to the soul. Of course not all people magically become wise and wonderful as they age, but those who choose to look at what they gain from advancing years, rather than what they lose, generally have a lustrous heart and a gleam in their eyes.

Ideally, the experiences accrued throughout the years bring increased wisdom and instill an inner security that allows us to speak our truth fearlessly and act from an unshakable sense of integrity. I love the quote from Dorothy Sayers: "Time and trouble will tame an advanced young woman, but an advanced old woman is uncontrollable by any earthly force." Yes. For the good of the whole, we need to be uncontrollable and untamed in our efforts to invite the spirit of love to quench the thirst of our souls and re-green our world.

I saw the beauty of aging exemplified by nature while on my trip to Arches National Park. In silent meditation, I sat in the protective shade of an eons-old rock that I came to think of as "Grandmother Rock." Gazing through the unbelievably huge arch in her facing sister, I was awed by the beauty created as this stone adapted to the elements and, over the millennium, grew a window through which the pristine sky gleams.

In the face of her patient transformation from one kind of beauty to another, I found myself asking how I was being called to mature as I age. What sandy sediment within me needs to erode away? What window into my very soul is yearning to be revealed in my walled-in personal world? What must be transformed in me in order for my transparency to reveal a vast and changing sky? I have no answers, only the knowledge that they will come if I remain open to the questions.

I am thankful for the wisdom, experience, and acceptance gleaned through aging.

I am an outrageous and untamed champion of love and learning.

Filling the Well

. . . .

A DRY WELL IRRIGATES NOTHING. IF WE ARE to be gloriously and outrageously alive, as Hildegaard of Bingen encourages us at the beginning of this section, we need to fill our inner wells regularly.

I love the metaphor, "God is an underground river, ever present and constantly flowing within and around us." But, even if we believe in an eternal river, do we take the time to fill our wells from it, or do we allow them to go dry?

Although the source is the same, the ways in which we fill our wells are unique and individual. What fills your well of spirit? What fills your well of emotion and physical well-being?

Close your eyes for a moment and allow a picture of a well to come into your mind's eye. Without judgment, explore your well. Is it full? How do you feel about it? What, if anything, does it need from you? Cleaning? Rebuilding? Take a few minutes to recreate it in a way that appeals to you. Perhaps you want your well to be the focal point of a beautiful garden or to stand in the midst of a clearing of majestic redwoods. Trust the images that your wise subconscious presents.

When your well pleases you, allow it to open to receive the pure waters of the eternal underground river of God. At the same time, begin to fill it from the top with those things that you know will fill your reservoirs to overflowing, such as giving yourself permission to have a free day with no obligations or demands, either internal or external. Do this until your well is brimming with pristine water.

After you've filled your well, take a little time to list those things that you can do to tap into the river of God and to fill your well yourself. Make a life-enhancing promise to yourself to do the things that will fill your well. Although a dry well irrigates nothing, a full well irrigates effortlessly.

I deserve to be filled to the brim.
I allow God's energy to flow through me.

Embodying
Heart Energy

The heart is the hub of all sacred places.
Go there and roam in it.

—Sri Nityananda

OUR HEARTS ARE POWERFUL SAGES which embody the wisdom, intuition, and compassion of the ages. They *know*, on a soul level, what is loving and nurturing, and they also deeply understand what connects us to the Divine. Given the chance, our hearts have the ability not only to help us become more loving but also to find fulfillment, peace of mind, increased creativity, and optimum health.

Intuitively, both the enlightened and the ordinary among us have known that love's transformative power can actually conquer all, and we believe that our hearts speak a different, more caring language than do our minds. But being believers doesn't automatically make us doers. Activating the power of our hearts takes practice and consistent intention, but we can tap into the mysterious energy of love for which our spirits thirst.

Realizing God's Love

. . . .

IT GIVES ME GREAT COMFORT TO BELIEVE that there never was, and never will be, a time when my essence was not beloved by God. As the wonderful mystic, Julian of Norwich, suggested when she said, "Between God and the soul, there is no between," I've come to realize that the distance I can feel between myself and God is not created by Her but by me. She is ever present, the pure emanation of heart-energy, attempting to love me into the awareness that I, too, am, in essence, heart-energy.

One of our most important spiritual tasks is to come to the realization of God's unending and unconditional love. The security of knowing that God loves us is the cornerstone of our soul-growth. As Anne Morrow Lindbergh said, "The most exhausting thing in life . . . is being insecure." Insecurity *is* exhausting, because it's riddled with fear and, therefore, barricades us from our hearts. Fear and love cannot coexist, and so, when we are in a state of fear, we cannot access the love that surrounds us constantly.

For many of us, this love is hard to experience. To give you a sense of security with God, the Beloved, allow yourself to close your eyes and imagine that you are in a beautiful place where you feel comfortable and accepted. Rest in the peace of your place. Begin to breathe deeply, in through your nose and out through your mouth. With each inhalation, draw into your heart a feeling of well-being, and as you exhale give yourself permission to breathe out any feelings of stress or uneasiness.

As you become more relaxed, notice that you are holding in your arms someone whom you genuinely love. It may be a baby or child, a pet, or a loved one. Breathe into your heart and allow love to flow from it to the other person's heart. After a few minutes, very gently change places and feel yourself being held in the lap of a benevolent presence who loves you deeply and unconditionally. If this is difficult for you, without judgment, become the holder again and pour love from your heart onto the person being held. Feel the outpouring of love surround you as it enfolds them. Slowly allow the picture to alter and imagine yourself feeling loved as you nestle in the welcoming lap of God.

Before the beginning God loved me.

God is loving me now.

Cleansing Our Hearts

. . . .

OUR HEARTS NOT ONLY ENCOMPASS THE strongest and wisest aspects of our nature, but also the softest and most vulnerable ones as well. Because life can be difficult, our hearts may become encrusted with feelings of fear and disillusionment or stained by sorrow and self-deprecating beliefs. Even if our lives have been utterly smooth, without a single pebble upon our path, we may have at least gathered a little dust along the way.

Because Spirit moves more freely through a clear heart, we can best embody heart energy when we cleanse our hearts. Doing so will provide an unobstructed passage through which God's love can flow.

When you can find a few quiet moments—even if it is before falling asleep tonight or arising tomorrow morning—tenderly perform a heart-check. With your eyes closed, place your hands over your heart and tell it that you love it. Sincerely thank your heart for its absolute faithfulness. Now see or sense the condition of your heart. Trust your wise intuition; whatever appears is probably the perfect symbol for you right now. Does it look clean? Does it feel clear?

If not, ask what you can do right now to cleanse and heal your heart. Honor the answer, even if it seems strange.

The last time I meditated on this, my heart was a little sad and had a small bruise at the tip. It was appreciative of my caring and wanted to be bathed in warm sea water and then have a poultice of lotus leaves applied to the bruise.

In the theater of my mind, I went to a favorite Hawaiian beach where the surf is gentle and soothing. Effortlessly floating in the warm, tropical water, I imagined it flowing through me, gently caressing and buoying up my heart. As a lotus drifted toward me, I held its pink leaves to my chest and asked that they heal the bruised area and cleanse my heart.

I cleanse and clear my heart when it needs it.

I invite the Spirit to flow easily through my heart.

Opening Our Hearts

. . . .

LOVE IS NOT MEANT TO BE HELD IN A clenched heart. Like water, love must be allowed to flow naturally and freely or it becomes grabby and turns into attachment and dependence. Fear is usually the icy fist that seizes our heart, clanging it closed. When our heart is locked behind iron doors, we're cut off from its innate wisdom and compassion, both of which are necessary for us to feel truly happy and fulfilled.

For our heart to be willing and able to open, we must dispel its fear and protect it from harm. Although no one can really wound our heart unless we allow it, fear keeps us from realizing that fact. As a wily adversary, fear is most easily transformed by the light of creative visualization.

Some of the visualizations that I and my clients use to allay fears include: seeing and feeling the hands of Christ over our hearts brushing away danger; putting on a magic, impermeable cloak; surrounding our hearts in an orb of white light; placing an invisible filter between ourselves and another; and being shielded by an angel.

It doesn't matter what you choose, only that it works for you. One whimsical client of mine imagines herself riding a huge white unicorn into tricky situations. If a barb or fear flies her way, her unicorn snags it on his magical horn and flings it harmlessly away. She knows that humor and fun help disperse fear.

Design a visualization that makes you feel safe and secure and relax into it. As you enjoy your personal mind-movie, begin to breathe more and more deeply. Invite any heart-closing fears to parade by and watch as your protectors render them impotent. Still surrounded by protection, visualize your heart opening in its perfect, right time and way. As it opens, feel the security and well-being flowing into it as you inhale, and feel that same sense of well-being flowing out to the world as you exhale. In and out. Gently, lovingly, and safely.

I protect my heart.

From my open heart flows pure love.

Cradling a Wounded Heart

. . . .

DURING AN EXTREMELY PAINFUL TIME IN MY life, I vowed to never be hurt that badly again. To protect myself, I armored my heart so effectively that it felt as if it began to atrophy from lack of use. Only with my children did I feel safe enough to give and receive love. Thank goodness—for without those kids, my soul might have withered and wafted away.

Luckily, my spirit began to rebel against its ever-increasing grayness and encouraged me to choose love rather than reclusive safety. At first I refused and huddled resolutely behind my armor. There must have been some spark of willingness within me for, as Spirit persisted, caring and helpful people began to appear in my life.

Annabelle, a wonderful woman who would become my spiritual mother, was an important guide. Knowing that I had an advocate whom I could call if I were desperate gave me the courage to creep around the corner of my armor and begin to heal my heart. The transformation process was neither fast nor easy but began to happen as soon as I started cradling my wounded heart.

As you would to an injured child, I crooned to my heart that everything would be okay, that I would protect and nurture it, that I would keep it as safe as possible. When I was too weak to be nurturing, I visualized my mother, Annabelle, an angel, or Mary, Christ's mother, holding the wounded part of me in soothing, comforting arms and infusing my heart with healing energy. During times when I was too bottomed-out to do anything myself, I called a friend and asked her to hold me in her prayers.

If your heart is wounded, console and comfort it, and don't hesitate to reach out to others for help in doing so.

I hold my heart in the gentle arms of love.

I allow others to help me heal.

Growing a Grinch Heart

. . . .

HEART-CENTERED THINKERS KNOW INTUI-
tively that love is power. As Anne Morrow
Lindbergh wrote, "Love is a force . . . it is not a
result; it is a cause. It is not a product; it pro-
duces. It is a power, like money, or steam, or
electricity. It is valueless unless you can give
something else by means of it."

As mentioned in the introduction, science is
now underscoring our intuitive awareness with
measurable data. One Institute of HeartMath
study that appealed to me shows that our hearts
are the strongest amplifying system we have for
generating positive electrical fields. When sub-
jects in the laboratory brought their attention
to their hearts and augmented that attention
with feelings of appreciation and caring, computer printouts displayed greatly increased
fields of energy emanating from their hearts in
ever-widening circles.

The picture HeartMath has drawn of this
phenomenon reminded me of Dr. Seuss' story
of *The Grinch Who Stole Christmas*. The Grinch's
heart was finally touched by the Whos in
Whoville, when they still exhibited the spirit of

Christmas even after all of their gifts and decorations had been stolen. Feeling what I guess was amazement and appreciation for the Whos, the Grinch's heart grew from a tiny dried up tidbit into a radiantly beautiful starburst filling his entire chest. Rays of heart-energy poured from him toward the little Whos happily singing below.

All of us can grow a Grinch heart. Quietly close your eyes and focus your attention on your heart area. Bring into your awareness a sense of deep appreciation for a person or situation. Bask in the resultant feelings and allow your heart to expand. See and feel your heart-energy amplified and enlarged, blessing you first, and then moving out to grace others with the gift of love.

Love is truly a force for good, and we can amplify our output.

My heart is continuously growing.

I give love graciously.

Roaming in the Heart

．．

So OFTEN WE ALLOW OUR MINDS TO ROAM
in areas that are not conducive to feeling good.
We ramble around in the past in hopes of a better yesterday, and then we leap ahead and
scurry fretfully around in the "what ifs" of the
future. As a consequence, most of us spend very
little time in the present moment, tuned into
what is going on right now.

One particularly destructive mind habit—
one of my own major weaknesses—is to rehash
and relive negative emotional experiences,
gnawing them, and our nerves, to shreds. Not
good, because five minutes of ruminating on an
argument creates the same imbalance in the au-
tonomic nervous system as does real-time
anger, and it depletes the immune system for
several hours afterward. Roaming in emotional
mine fields is bad for our physical, emotional,
and spiritual health.

Diametrically opposed to the effects we get
from straying into negativity are the positive effects received by roaming in the fields of our
heart, the "hub of all sacred places" according to
Sri Nityananda. Here we learn to be present to
what is, right now, without being mired in the

past or grasping for the future. Find a quiet moment today and allow your body to settle into a comfortable position. Encourage your body to soften, your breath to deepen, and your mind to be still. Focus on your breath and watch as it automatically begins to slow down. Bring your attention to your heart. Feel gratitude and admiration for it.

As you relax, create a beautiful scene that is symbolic of your heart. If the picture that first appears doesn't appeal to you, let it fade and create a new one. Explore your heartscape; deeply enjoy and appreciate what it generously offers. Be open to surprise blessings that may arise. You can invite those whom you love to join you, or you may prefer to have a solitary experience. Whatever you choose, trust the intuition of your heart to provide a scene that is right for you now.

During the day, refresh yourself by taking minute-vacations to come into the present moment. Return to the sacred hub of your heart and roam in it.

My heart is sacred.

I am worthy of a heartscape that is beautiful and refreshing.

Soothing Our Hearts

. . . .

BECAUSE WE KNOW BEST WHEN OUR SPIRITS have been mowed down by a Mac truck, or merely nicked by a moped, it's up to us to soothe our hearts and souls and be willing to ask for soothing from others.

While out on the road promoting *Heart Centered Marriage*, my heart gave me ample evidence that it needed some lovin' care. It was one of those days that you'd like to erase from the calendar, culminating with a talk I gave at a large bookstore. Six people showed up; one was a heckler and two (including my own escort) fell asleep, and, even worse, only two books were sold at the end of my presentation. My heart felt as if it were petrifying inside my chest and I could scarcely breathe. By the time I limped back to my hotel, I was the lowest of the low.

I called my husband and a friend for support and neither were home. "See, you're not even important to *them!*" wailed a vulnerable inner voice before a wiser, more mature, message could make itself heard and said, "Looks like you're on your own for this one, Toots. Practice what you preach."

First, as if it were a cherished baby, I held my book over my heart and told it that it was very, very good. You can do this with any creation or idea of yours. Our creations carry an energy that links with our own. As we reassure them, we reassure ourselves. Then I did the following exercise. If you've had a recent disappointment, or felt badly about yourself for some reason, you too might benefit from it.

With your hands over your heart, pour love into your heart and to the part of you that feels inadequate or upset. Gently soothe your heart with consoling affirmations such as, "I love you. I honor you. You are a wonderful and loving heart. I value you. I take care of you. I listen to you, and I will protect you."

We all have vulnerable aspects of our being that need to be soothed on occasion. It is our sacred charge to comfort our hurting hearts.

I compassionately soothe my aching heart.

I love and comfort my vulnerable selves.

Surrendering Head to Heart

FOR CENTURIES THE HEAD HAS RULED THE roost. "I think therefore I am" has been the credo of our left-brain-dominated society, and, as a consequence, the whole world is out of balance. Individually and universally, we need to return to the balance and harmony that can be achieved only by training our heads to surrender to the wisdom and compassion of our hearts.

When I broached this subject to Martha, a client of mine who is a very business-oriented realtor, she paled and said, "Sue, you can't be serious! If I follow my heart I won't be able to survive in this competitive, dog-eat-dog field." I told her that I didn't think her fears would materialize and, skeptically, she agreed to do the following meditation for about three minutes each morning until I saw her again in two weeks.

At her next appointment, Martha's fears were somewhat quieted. She told me, "Well, I didn't *lose* any business, but I didn't *gain* any either! I have noticed a funny thing. I feel less stressed and my clients seem to have gotten nicer." My bet is that Martha, herself, is sending out a calmer heart frequency that makes her clients feel more comfortable around her. That's not only good for her, but it's also good for business.

You too can benefit from the balance between heart and head. With your eyes closed, breathe deeply into your heart area and feel it accepting and absorbing the life-giving infusion. Imagine that your heart is expanding and that loving energy is flowing from its center like circles on the surface of a pond. With reverence, physically bow your head toward your heart. Even if it feels awkward, silently tell your heart that your head wishes to cooperate with it, surrender to it, and serve it. Ask your heart's inherent wisdom and love to guide you.

My head surrenders to my heart.

My heart is a wise and compassionate guide.

Softening in the Face of Hardness

. . . .

CAMILLA HAD MADE A PROMISE TO HERSELF that, as a part of her spiritual discipline, she would learn to soften her responses, attitudes, and judgments. Because she was prone to feeling defensive when faced with difficult situations or people, she decided to use such events as reminders to soften. Right off the bat, her husband (our mates are always such good teachers) provided her with the perfect opportunity when he surprisingly overreacted to a suggestion she made.

Feeling as if she'd been kicked in the stomach, Camilla nonetheless remembered that here was an opportunity to soften. Although she managed to keep her response quiet, her judgments where flaring inside and her heart felt hard and constricted. She excused herself and went to a private place where she attempted to tune into her heart. Quieting her mind was like wrestling with a two year old in the midst of a temper tantrum, but finally she was able to get in touch with her heart. First she comforted and forgave the person within her who felt hurt, frustrated, and angry. When she was calmer, she asked her heart what to do in this situation. The answer was an unequivocal, "Relax and back off."

Relaxing and backing off while there was a rift between herself and her husband was not exactly Camilla's first choice or best talent, but she did as her heart suggested. Later that evening, her patience was rewarded when her husband told her that he had had a troublesome business reversal right before their flare-up. Intuitively she realized that this was his way of explaining his reaction and that an escalation of bad feelings between them had been avoided by her backing off.

Although it's often difficult to do, softening in the face of hardness allows us to return to our hearts where true strength and peace of mind reside.

I can be safe and soft at the same time.

Faced with hardness, I remember to soften.

Weaving Essence and Experience

. . . .

OUR ESSENCE IS SPIRIT, AND OUR EXPERIENCE
is human. Therefore, while our essence is always love, our experiences can be ragged,
flawed, or downright icky. The trick is to infuse
experience with essence and weave them together, for it is through our very humanness in
conjunction with Spirit that our soul grows. We
need not subjugate nor negate our humanness
in order to become a vessel of love, but rather
become the best human we can be. Through
love and acceptance, we can transform our
human limitations into a clear window through
which our essence can shine. Healing, honing,
and honoring our humanity encourages us to
become the best possible vehicle for the light of
Spirit.

Because her husband is a football fan and she
likes to participate in activities with him, Sylvia
has learned to transform the experience of
going to a football game into a spiritual opportunity. Silently fuming about what a stupid and
dangerous sport football was used to ruin the
outings for Sylvia, but now she sends love and
protective light to all of the players. In weaving

her essence into football experiences, she is also creating a stronger bond with her husband.

Play with the concept of weaving for a minute. Close your eyes and relax and, in whatever way feels right to you, give yourself permission to create a fanciful tapestry of your life. Imagine a color or colors for both your essence and your experience. You can choose one particular experience or focus on experiences in general. Anything is perfectly alright.

Ask both the wisdom and the whimsy of your heart to help weave the colors of essence and experience together in a symbolic picture. What do you love about the weaving? What do you dislike, or what makes you uncomfortable?

Study your tapestry as you would a dream. There are undoubtedly valuable hints in this meditation about how you feel you're doing with the task of weaving essence and experience together. As we become more adept at bringing our essence into everyday experiences, they will be magically transformed into everyday blessings.

I accept and honor both my essence and my experiences.

Bathed in love, all experiences can become blessings.

Lightening Up

. . . .

HUMOR IS A WONDERFUL HEART ENERGY, A proven leavening agent. Without humor, our lives become increasingly colorless and drab. Yet in our hectic daily schedules, it's easy to let obligation and frustration drain our humor veins, leaving us with a pallor becoming only to an android or a vampire.

One of the best ways to invite humor back into our lives and spark up our spirits is to be in the presence of children and to really pay attention to them. If little ones aren't available to you, see if you can find a playmate in the child within yourself and encourage her to help you lighten up.

Janie, a dear friend of mine, was inching along in traffic, totally frustrated. Every now and then she'd hit the steering wheel muttering something akin to, "Come *on!!!*" Finally, from the backseat, her beautiful, angelic-looking two-year-old daughter piped up with a suggestion, "Say fuggum, Mommy!" Nonplussed, but thoroughly amused, Janie felt her spirits immediately lift. Delight and appreciation for her daughter's unintended wit opened her heart, causing traffic to take a backseat to love and laughter. For years, Janie and I would say, "Just say *fuggum*, Mommy!" to each other when we were crabby.

As Art Linkletter well knew, kids say the darndest things, and those wee wisdoms often help us laugh ourselves to lightness. We always have our internal kid-comedian with us, and it will help us immeasurably if we can encourage her to feel free to say the darndest things to us. The car is a great place to practice for two reasons; traffic *is* frustrating, and no one can hear our silliness.

This may seem frivolous to you, but it really isn't. Any means we can employ to embody more heart energy and lighten up our lives are good. Young children and healed inner children are natural sources of heartful—not hurtful—humor. Take some time today to do something impractical and fun.

I laugh easily and naturally.

I encourage my inner kid to come out and play.

Bearing Beams of Love

. . . .

WE ARE HERE TO DO GOOD. TO LIVE OUT our spiritual purpose, we are called to appreciate, honor, empower, and listen to ourselves and to others who speak to us: To be the good we are meant to be. Poet William Blake stated this sentiment beautifully when he wrote, "We are here but for a little while to learn to bear the beams of love."

Beams of love originate in and emanate from our hearts. Our hearts are individual, internal wisdom teachers consistently nudging us toward a higher degree of consciousness and more ability to love.

Ancient sages reside within our hearts bearing torches from which the beams of love flow. They welcome our calls for counsel and guidance.

It often helps to have a visual reference on which to draw when thinking about our heart teachers. Toward that end, please close your eyes and use any technique that works for you to move into a restful state of mind. In your mind's eye, see yourself seated at a beautiful campfire in the gathering dusk. Ask your heart to provide you with a picture or sense of the teacher, or teachers, who reside within in it. Invite them to share the light of your fire. If you don't feel loved by and safe with the ones who come, erase them and repeat the invitation. When the appropriate teachers appear, bask in their presence. Present them with any questions that come to your mind. Listen carefully. Answers may be heard, sensed intuitively, or seen as symbols. At the end of your time together, ask your teachers how best to communicate with them in the future. Thank them for appearing.

I listen to the wisdom of my heart's sages.
I send forth beams of light and love.

Being Truly Nice

I RECENTLY MET JILL, A YOUNG WOMAN WHO is a joy to be around. Everyone loves her and gravitates toward her. I can see why, because she is genuinely nice to each person she encounters. Recently I watched her interact with Priscilla, her difficult-to-get-along-with mother-in-law.

While Priscilla was grumping about something—a fairly consistent habit of hers—Jill silently reached over and stroked her arm. No judgment, just an accepting presence. During the entire weekend I was in her company, I never heard Jill say anything that wasn't upbeat. Consequently, we all felt good around her— safe, seen, even savored.

Niceness sometimes connotes wimpiness, but that interpretation usually comes from the fact that many of us have felt that it was expected of us to *make* nice even when we didn't *feel* nice. When we realize that niceness is a natural outgrowth of deep kindness and caring, we can consciously choose to develop our niceness quotient. We can set our intention to truly *being* nice, rather than putting on a phony nice front.

Often, the simple desire to grow our soul through niceness helps us focus on coming from our hearts where true niceness flourishes.

It's perfectly okay to act nice even when we don't feel it as long as we're doing so from personal choice, not from a sense of obligation or fear. Freely choosing to act nice will actually help us begin to embody the authentic niceness of our hearts.

Nice not only *wears* well, but, generally, it also *fares* well, for kindness is never out-of-date nor out-of-style and is welcome in all circles. Everyone enjoys being uplifted in the safe haven of nice attitudes and actions. Being truly nice, as Jill is, makes us a heart-lifter.

I choose to act in kind and caring ways.

I am a heart-lifter.

Inviting Intuition In

INTUITION IS KNOWING WHAT WE KNOW without knowing how we know it. Because intuition is perceiving and understanding without conscious reasoning, it's a shortcut to learning for us. It works so fast that our minds need time to figure out what our intuitive hearts know immediately.

Because we live in a society that is so focused on the knowledge that comes from our heads, our task as we seek a stronger connection to Spirit is to have the courage to trust the intuitive voice that whispers to us. As we learn to trust our intuition and invite it more fully into our awareness, it will breathe a sigh of relief and say, "Ah, good. I've been waiting here in your heart to be recognized and relied on."

The beauty of intuition is that it is smarter than any problem and comes from a much higher source than does opinion. Intuition is more grounded in ancient wisdom and its input comes from realms other than the conscious. Opinion is colored by many brushes, but intuition comes from the heart and is untainted by outside influence.

Just a year ago, my husband Gene's intuition saved me untold heartache. He was scheduled to leave the house early one morning and be gone most of the day on errands, but he felt uneasy about leaving and stalled his departure. Hesitation is exceedingly unusual for him, but it soon became clear that his intuition was warning him that he would be needed at home. Right before he was about to force himself out the door, my sister called to say that my father had had a heart attack. Because Gene was home and is great at logistics and arranging travel, I was able to make it to Dad's side in time to have a meaningful "I love you, goodbye" conversation before he died. Thank God that Gene invited his intuition into his awareness! My heart is so much better off because he listened to his.

You, too, regularly receive nudges from your heart. By listening, you invite the wisdom of intuition into your life.

I listen to my heart's whispers.
My intuition is wise and trustworthy.

Freeing the Spirit of
Peace and Love

. . . .

*Peace and love are alive in us, but we are
not always alive in peace and love.*
　　　　　　—Julian of Norwich

RETURNING TO OUR HEARTS IS SUCH A
simple concept that we may feel tempted to
downplay its significance but we mustn't, because a conscious return to our hearts frees the
spirit of love and peace within us. And each of
us—as well as the world as a whole—is thirsting
for the solace of living within the safety and
serenity of love and peace.

When our hearts are ignored, they become
crusted over, which naturally cuts peace and
love out of our day-to-day life. Within a ne-
glected heart, the spirit of love is imprisoned,
unable to share its healing energy with us or all
the others who need it. By returning to our
hearts, we reclaim the Sacred Feminine Voice
whose values include not only peace and love
but also tolerance, acceptance, compassion, intuitive wisdom, cooperation, and complementa-
tion. Reinstating these heart-centered values

will not only enliven us but will also reap rich rewards for our children and our planet.

Gently close your eyes and pay attention to your heart area. In a few moments, begin to visualize a door behind which you will find your heart. Carefully, but without judgment, notice what the door looks like. If it is barricaded or blocked, ask for help from your guardian angel, or any wise guide that you relate to, to open it. Once inside, imagine that you are met by a radiantly strong and compassionate feminine being. In her hands she holds symbols for both peace and love. Question her about how you can bring these qualities alive within your life.

At the end of this meditation, it might be a good idea to make a note of the ideas you received from the Sacred Feminine Voice within your heart and post it as a reminder. Choosing to bring peace and love alive within ourselves by coming from our hearts on a consistent basis is the hope of the world.

The spirit of peace and love is strong and free within me.

I listen to my Sacred Feminine Voice.

Siphoning Off Stress

. . . .

ONE OF THE WAYS WE TEND TO SLIP FROM our loving hearts into our reactive guts is to become overwhelmed by stress. A little stress is necessary to create some get-up-and-go, but too much can overpower us and short out our circuits. Stress is the four-letter word of our time. Who hasn't felt stressed out, tension-ridden, and temper-tattered at one time or another? How can we siphon off the excess stress that blocks our ability to live from our hearts?

There are many short-term stress-busters such as drinking, overeating, and being bitchy that we want to avoid because they are unhealthy and create shame and strained relationships. Healthily siphoning off excess stress is a three-fold process.

First, we need to become mentally aware of the stress and let it go before it reaches red-alert status. Second, it's important to physically release pent-up energy. Our bodies, like sponges, sop up tension into all of the their nooks and crannies. Screaming is a good physical release as long as it's not aimed at anyone and is done in private (screams can be muffled with a towel or pillow). Taking a run or brisk walk, beating a bed with a tennis racket, digging ferociously in the garden, and whacking tennis balls are all great stress siphons. You will know what's best for you. As long as physical release is not detrimental to yourself or anyone else, it usually helps clear a path to the heart.

Allowing our hearts to transform stress is the third step in siphoning it out of our bodies and souls. Move your awareness to your heart and visualize a symbol for the stress. Let the light and love of Spirit pour through you onto your symbol. Allow it to be transformed into peaceful energy. If it won't change, encase it in a container and put it on a remote shelf, and then surround yourself with a protective shield of light.

I am aware of stress and release it constructively.

I take stress into my heart, and bless and transform it with love and light.

Nourishing
Our Souls

It is only when we can believe that we are creating the soul that life has any meaning, but when we can believe it—and I do and always have—then there is nothing we do that is without meaning and nothing that we suffer that does not hold the seed of creation in it.

—May Sarton

WE EACH SEEK UNITY OF BODY, mind, and spirit. As fundamentally spiritual beings living increasingly fragmented lives, we—even if we're not consciously aware of it—yearn to join the essentially complementary aspects of our being and integrate them into a balanced whole. I believe this yearning comes from deep within our souls as a memory of our life-purpose, which is that of achieving union between woman, who is finite, and spirit, which is infinite.

In order to have reconciliation of our human and spirit selves, both must be nourished and nurtured, befriended and given a voice. It is through the cleansed window of our humanity that our souls shine and become ever more visible. Because our humanity is loud and insistent while our spirit is quiet and patient, in the short run it's easier to "hop to" the worldly, physical demands and slight the whispers emanating from our spiritual selves. But, eventually, most of us, motivated by either a burning desire or an intermittent malaise, turn our attention to our souls and begin to heed their wisdom.

Daring to Breathe

. . . .

DARING TO BREATHE IS ACTUALLY DARING TO live. As we all know, when we cease breathing, we die. As long as we are alive, the depth of our breathing determines the amount of life force we bring into ourselves. Given only a stingy amount of oxygen, our bodies, hearts, and minds will not function well.

When we are experiencing stress of any kind, our breathing has a tendency to get very shallow. As a therapist, I often need to remind my clients to breathe when they are working on issues. Often deeper breathing brings a release of tears and tension.

I was grateful the other day to notice a one-word bumper sticker: BREATHE, it prompted. *Breathe* is a reminder we need to give ourselves regularly. Breathing deeply brings more energy into our bodies, which, in turn, helps clarify both our thoughts and feelings.

Daring to breathe nourishes our souls as well. Almost all creation myths have God making man/woman from the soil of the earth and animating him/her by breathing into his/her nostrils the "breath of life." It's no wonder then that the words *soul* and *spirit* originated from *anima* and *spiritus*, both of which mean "breath." Through the grace of God, we breathe, and it is the breath of God that we breathe. I find it very comforting to believe that God is as near to me as my next breath.

For the next five minutes, give yourself the life-enhancing gift of intentional breathing. With eyes closed, breathe deeply in through your nose, taking the breath of God—down, down into the center of your belly. Exhale completely through your mouth. As you inhale, imagine pure energy flowing in to nourish body and soul. As you exhale, let go of all that you would like to release.

If you get nothing else from *The Woman's Book of Spirit,* I encourage you to make a commitment to breathe deeply five minutes a day—perhaps right before you get up or go to sleep. I think you'll be surprised and pleased at the profound changes that can occur from this one thing. Dare to do it!

Breathe!

I nourish body and soul by breathing deeply.

Going Where Gaia
Soothes Your Soul

. . . .

IT FEEDS OUR SPIRITS TO HAVE SPECIAL
places where Gaia, Mother Nature, can infuse
us with her renewing energy. For me, it's the
beach. While there, thoughts recede and wor-
ries abate. I could almost hang an UNOCCU-
PIED sign on my mind or stamp NOT AT THIS
ADDRESS on my physical self. Even though I
may not feel as if I've thought of a thing, as a result of being by the water, questions are often
answered and decisions clarified. It's as if I've
been mesmerized out of my own way, thereby
freeing my spirit to do its wiser work.

Not all the insights that come up are peaches
and cream. At the ocean, Gaia invites me to experience and release difficult feelings, especially
grief—not as a head-trip, but rather at a more
primal, accepting-the-natural-cycle-of-things way.
Joy comes similarly. It's as if my soul gently surfs
the waves and the movement quiets my human
self. No matter what I feel or don't feel, I return
from a time at the beach revived and rejuve-
nated. For me, a trip to the ocean is a trip to the
eternal spring within myself.

Consider for a moment where your soul rests most easily. Where do you feel infinitely safe and return from replenished? What place in Mother Nature allows you to most readily hear the intuitive wisdom of your heart and seamlessly heal from searing wounds? It can be as exotic as a Polynesian beach or as accessible as your backyard. Even if you've only been to your special place once, you can always return in your imagination. If you don't have a sacred space in nature, be on the lookout for one and, until you find it, create one in your mind's eye.

Take a few quiet moments now to allow Gaia to nourish your soul. Imagine yourself in a grace-filled place and, as free of thought as possible, absorb the soothing energy. Breathe, relax, bask in nature's blessing.

I allow Gaia to soothe my soul.

Thank you, Mother Nature, for your blessings.

Being Our Own Lamp

AS HE WAS DYING, THE BUDDHA SAID, "Be a lamp unto yourself." I think he was challenging us to become aware of our spiritual essence, to read ourselves by our *own* light, to follow the path that resonates with our own hearts and minds right here, right now. As we recognize own unique light, we can choose to shine it on the people and places that need illuminating. For the good of the world, as well as our own personal good, it's vital that we tip over the proverbial bushel and become aware of the beautiful and distinctive light we have been given to share.

Settle yourself into a comfortable place and position and allow your breath to deepen naturally. With each breath, any tension that you are feeling begins to wane, drifting lazily and effortlessly out of your body as you exhale. The more you relax, the more you sink into the darkness behind your eyelids—a safe, embracing, womblike darkness wrapping around you like a soft comforter.

Stay here, safe and warm in the velvety darkness, as long as you like. At the right time for you, notice, in the distance, a small pinpoint of light. Gently and leisurely move toward the faint glow. Coming closer, you see that the light is emanating from an exquisite lamp resting atop a lamp stand. If you don't like the lamp that you see, allow it to fade and be replaced by one that feels right to you. Realizing that the lamp is a symbol of your unique inner light brought forth by your wise subconscious, ask it to share its wisdom with you. Listen carefully.

By the light of many lamps, much can be illuminated.

I am my own best light.
I share my love and light.

Resting in the Cradle
of Friendship

. . . .

IN ORDER FOR HER SPIRIT TO SOAR, A WOMAN needs the sense of security that close friendships provide. We need to be known and accepted for who we are and, at the same time, gently encouraged to become who we have the potential to be. When the soft feathers of friendship cradle our weary heads, we rest more easily and arise refreshed and ready to grow.

Ruth and Anne have been dear friends for almost twenty years. Although now separated by miles, they are committed to remaining united by fax, phone, and visits. Why is their connection so important to them? Because they truly *know* each other. Even though secrets and shame have been shared as readily as silliness and successes, their love and delight in each other continues to mature and ripen as they do.

"Sometimes I'm just starved to talk to and be with someone who knows me as well as I know them," Ruth once told Anne. She was voicing a common yearning in women. Being feminine, our ability to really know others often comes fairly naturally. It is one of our gifts, but a gift that we need to receive as well as give. We, too, need to be known. Being truly *known* and accepted, as is, can nourish our soul to new heights.

Right now, give yourself the gift of thinking about the special friendships that nourish you. Do you see or talk to these people enough to feel nourished? If you feel the lack of such trusted friendship, creatively play with what you can you do to reach out and meet new people. It's perfectly okay to make a plan. Perhaps write a list of friends whom you would like to connect with more regularly and decide how to do so. Pencil them in and then follow through. You can make another plan for fostering new connections.

You will feel better when you fill the need to nourish yourself with the "soul food" of friendship.

I have a right to be known and accepted as I truly am.

I give myself the gift of friendship.

Culling Complications,
Welcoming Simplicity

. . . .

WE ARE CONTINUALLY SEDUCED BY SOCIETY
and our own need to do more, earn more, and
spend more into continuously complicating our
lives. Although some high-powered activity is
stimulating, even fun, and sometimes necessary,
too much is numbing and debilitating. The
price many of us pay for an overcomplicated existence is poor health, loss of serenity, fractured
relationships, and an unspoken lament of, "Is
this all there is?"

As a result of hard work and business acumen, the company Sarah and her husband
started in their garage grew beyond their
wildest imaginings. With the growth, Sarah's responsibilities increased, her private time all but
ceased, and she had no opportunity for relaxation. She assured herself and friends that she
was going to slow down—right after this next
trip, the coming ad campaign, or ad infinitum. .
. . It wasn't until she woke up one morning in
excruciating pain, her shoulders and arms immobile, that Sarah realized she had to make
changes. She simply couldn't "shoulder" all the

responsibilities she was carrying. Complication was literally crippling her.

Sarah still works more than is totally comfortable, but she is also learning to delegate, set priorities, and simplify. She hired some help, turned down some projects, and pruned some acquaintances who were energy drains. Her life now includes solitude, gardening, time for friends and family, a regular meditation group, and daily exercise, all of which nourish her soul.

With great love and respect for yourself, gently but with absolute—and maybe life-saving—honesty, examine your life. Is it too complicated to be comfortable? If so, where can you simplify? What small step can you take today to welcome simplicity into your days and serenity into your nights?

A simpler life is frequently a more satisfying life.

I take responsibility for simplifying my life.
I am able to cull out complications.

Quieting the Mind

. . . .

IT IS IN THE SILENCE OF A QUIET MIND THAT
our spirits make themselves known to us. In the
tranquility of a calm mind, we become aware of
the murmurs of our soul and learn to appreciate
the wisdom of our hearts. Indra Devi, author of
Renewing Your Life Through Yoga, beautifully describes the quiet mind: "Like water, which can
clearly mirror the sky and the trees only so long
as its surface is undisturbed, the mind can only
reflect the true image of the Self when it is tranquil and wholly relaxed. A ghost of wind—and
the rippling waters will distort the reflection; a
storm—and the reflection disappears altogether."

We are living in stormy times in which winds
blow wildly across the waters of our minds and
can all but obliterate our spiritual essence. But I
know from personal experience that we can
quiet both the storms and our minds. When I
was younger, giant tsunamis regularly whipped
the waters of my mind into a frenzy, rendering
me deaf to my conscious wisdom, let alone the
wisdom of my heart and soul. Although storms
still ruffle my waters, remembering to breathe

deeply and doing the following meditation helps the tempest to subside.

Close your eyes and gently allow your breath to deepen. Breathe in the idea of serenity and peace, and breathe out chaos and confusion. In your mind's eye, imagine a pond or lake that symbolizes your mind. Without judgment, notice how calm or turbulent it is and observe it for a minute. Ask your wise inner knowing what you can learn from this disturbance, and quietly listen. It doesn't matter if you "hear" an answer, trust that you will be made aware when the time is right. Now, breathe into your heart and, very deliberately, still the wind across the water. Breathe deeply until the lake is tranquil. Look at your reflection and thank yourself for calming the storm.

A quiet mind can reflect the real you.

Each day I become calmer and clearer.

I am a clear reflection of the Divine Spirit.

Unplugging the Phone

. . . .

IN A MOVIE REVIEW I READ RECENTLY, THE reviewer said, "This movie shows that our world may not end with a bang or a whimper but with a busy signal." What an apt metaphor! Our lives are busy, our phones and faxes are busy, our kids are busy, our friends are busy, our mates are busy, and our minds are busy. With these interminable busy signals, how can our souls ever contact us?

Joni is a friend of mine who never answers the phone but lets the answering machine be her vigilant secretary. She says it saves her a tremendous amount of time and energy, because she is the one who decides when she feels like talking and can call people back when she's ready.

Unplugging the literal telephone may not be feasible—I for one am too curious to let the phone ring, and for many of us the phone is our livelihood. But what about the busy signals in our lives? Do our kids get a busy signal when they need our attention? How about the little kids we all carry around inside of us; can they get through to us? Very importantly, are the bearers of our intuitive, heart-wisdom able to get our attention, or are they, too, frustrated by a continuous busy signal?

Interestingly, the loudest, most incessant buzzers demanding our attention can also be the least nourishing to our souls, but we answer them out of habit or a sense of obligation. I'm sure you can think of a few annoying and energy wasting distractions. Solicitors who call during the dinner hour spring to mind. One simple way to eliminate some of the busyness from our lives is to "turn off the ringer" on superfluous demands. Doing so gives us more opportunity to connect with ourselves and those we love.

It may sound mundane, but unplugging from only a few distractions can make us feel much freer. Experiment by cutting the connection to only one thing that is an energy drain for you and see how it feels.

I eliminate the unimportant.

I have enough time and attention to give to that which is important to me.

Honoring Our Own Rhythm

. . . .

"I GOT RHYTHM, YOU GOT RHYTHM, ALL God's children got rhythm," declares the spiritual. True, but we women regularly allow ourselves to be pulled from our own rhythm into another's, and we are especially prone to subjugate our rhythm to those of our mates and children. Luckily, we are also incredibly adaptable and can modify our rhythm to others for fairly long periods of time without adverse effects.

However, endlessly disregarding our inner music eventually causes us to literally be out of step with ourselves. A few of the resultant feelings may be irritation, depression, restlessness, and resentment. When we experience these, it's time to dance to our own drummer and find ways to honor our unique rhythm.

I experienced being very out-of-sync not long ago. Worn out from long writing sessions and a burst of author-on-tour promotional trips, and thoroughly exhausted from emoting both in person and on paper, I was not my nicest person. Luckily for him, my husband had planned a trip out of town. Alone and assisted by a bout of food poisoning, my life slowed to about one-third of its normal pace.

I turned down most offers to socialize, but at one gathering that I needed to attend people commented on how "beautiful" I looked and wondered if I'd had plastic surgery. A rather backhanded compliment, but never having borne the label of beautiful—especially not since the "crone years" started—I accepted their comment gladly. Upon reflection, I think the beauty these people saw was a result of the relaxation, ease, and comfort I felt at being in my own rhythm for those few days.

We all need to rest, retreat, and replenish. Pay attention to your body and soul signals and find your own unique and precious rhythm, if not for days, then for hours or minutes today. What does paying attention to your rhythm teach you? Are there any small changes in yours that you could make to accommodate yourself? The rhythm to which our spirit can best dance is the rhythm of Self.

I know, appreciate, and allow my own rhythm.

Each day I take some time to be in my personal rhythm.

Tending the Temple

. . . .

OUR BODIES ARE AMAZINGLY MIRACULOUS temples that house our souls and allow us to have this existence. They are the vehicles through which we express ourselves while they instinctively perform trillions of functions that keep us up and running. But, like Rodney Dangerfield, they often "don't get no respect" from us.

As Walt Whitman made clear when he wrote, "If life and the soul are sacred, the human body is sacred," we need to realize the sanctity of our body-temple and make it a priority to tend to it responsibly and respectfully. When the body is too tired, malnourished, overworked, stressed out, or lacks enough exercise, it begins to falter system by system. Because the body/spirit connection is so strong, in some real sense, ignoring our body is a spiritual emergency; we have ravaged our temple.

Realizing our need to tend the temple is especially hard when we're in a caregiver role (and who of us is not, in some form or another?). Betty was the primary caretaker for her terminally ill husband. While she carefully prepared meals for him, she existed on snacks and coffee. Although she used to walk daily, she no longer felt she could leave the house unless it was on a necessary errand. Her daughter, visiting from out of town, was appalled at her mother's appearance. "You look worse than Dad!" she cried, and then set about helping Betty find regular help from her church and hospice. From her daughter's reaction, Betty learned an important lesson; taking care of Self is so easy to forget and so necessary to remember.

For a moment, close your eyes and visualize a temple that symbolizes your body right now. Don't be alarmed if it looks ramshackled. The first time I did this visualization, my temple looked like the remnants of an old treehouse. Learn from the image that your wise subconscious presents. Ask your temple what it wants and needs in order to feel healthy and energetic.

If our body houses our soul, can it peek through the clutter or get our attention amid the chaos?

I treat my body as I would a dear friend.
My body is the sacred temple of my soul.

Steering Clear of Black Holes

. . . .

I WAS TALKING TO A WISE YOUNG WOMAN named Laurie about relationships, and she made a statement that I've never forgotten: "I try to make sure that in all of my important relationships there is an even exchange of energy." Laurie's philosophy struck at the very heart of an issue I was wrestling with concerning a friendship with two women. I was usually with these women in a group of four, and I always felt weird during and after a gathering.

Laurie's comment came at the time when I was chastising myself harshly for feeling uncomfortable in these friendships. As a therapist, I know all about projection of our unconscious feelings onto other people, and I worked with myself about the possibility that I was doing that. But no little subconscious worms were unearthed in all of my digging, so I examined my feelings by the light of Laurie's statement and realized that there was no *exchange* of energy. The energy I put out to these two women was merely absorbed as if it had disappeared into a black hole and none came back to me.

There are some perfectly wonderful people who, mysteriously, are virtual black holes for our energy. We send scads of energy and attention their way, and it just disappears. Nothing comes back. Zero, zip! If we're saddled with the belief that everyone needs to like us in order for us to be acceptable or that we should be able to be friends with anyone, we can cause ourselves a lot of pain. We're simply "energetic misses" with some people. We're not bad, they're not bad; we just don't fit.

If you are in a relationship that feels one-sided and believe that you must continue it in order to be a nice person, for your own good let go of that belief. First, examine the possibility that you're projecting your "own stuff," and then trust your wise intuition. If it seems right, give yourself permission to move out of Black Hole Territory.

We have too little time to waste it in relationships that are not equal and mutually rewarding. *Exchanging* energy nourishes our souls—black holes enervate rather than energize them.

I choose relationships in which energy is exchanged equally.

It's perfectly okay not to hit it off with absolutely everyone.

Surrendering to Tiredness

. . . .

SURRENDER TO TIREDNESS! THE IDEA IS A tough one to assimilate, isn't it? Of course it is a hard concept to grasp, because it isn't the way we've been trained to act. It's true that women have incredible stamina and can do it all for a while, but there is the reality of accumulated fatigue. After a certain amount of outpouring, we are just plain bone-weary. To nourish both our souls and our bodies, we need to surrender to tiredness before it becomes exhaustion and our wise body has no recourse but to knock the pegs out from under us via illness, incompetence, or debilitating depression.

Not long after our daughter's wedding, I was feeling like a beige dishrag. No energy, no enthusiasm, no feelings of love; just a gray void. Longing to know why my zest for life was at zero and falling, I meditated and then wrote questions to whom I hoped would be the wise person within me. Two of my questions were: "Why don't I feel anything?" and "Why are there so many tears as I write this?"

The answer I wrote to myself was this: *The tears are tiredness. You have been holding—even mak-*

ing—the space for everyone in your family and extended family. You are allowed to rest. That is grace. Remember, even the church statues are draped during Holy Week. Even they are allowed to rest. So rest, my dear. This is your holy time, and much is synthesizing on different levels in dreams,and so on. Sit, rest, replenish. It was such a profound message for me that, even as I write this now, tears have welled up and I realize again how much I resist surrendering to tiredness.

If you are a woman who easily surrenders to tiredness, I congratulate you. If you are like me and find it difficult, then, together, let us give each other permission right now to rest and replenish in the perfect, right ways for us.

*I have the right and responsibility to rest
and replenish myself.*

I know when I am tired and allow myself to rest.

Sending Guilt Down the Drain

. . . .

GUILT SUCKS OUR SOULS DRY. A TINY TINGE of guilt can be appropriate and even helpful if we use it as a warning signal— "Whoops, wrong way. Wait, do I really want to say/do that?" But most of us use the guilt-as-sledge-hammer approach and let it bludgeon us until we're black and blue.

After a discussion with her new husband in which he told her that he was having a very hard time with her "freeloader" eighteen-year-old son, Marcie told the boy that he needed to move out. Almost immediately she was aware that she didn't want him to leave and that telling him to do so had been an attempt to appease her husband. On the heels of the ultimatum, Marcie and her husband went square dancing. "Well," she said, "Guilt can't dance!" How right she is. Guilt hobbles us almost more than any emotion, and 94 percent (I just made that number up, but I'm probably close) of the guilt we take on is either inappropriate or not ours in the first place. Guilt-grabbing is one of women's lesser talents.

Alice, a client of mine and a recovering guilt-grabber, shared a wonderful ritual with me that she came up with as a part of her self-therapy. When she notices that she is "slimed with guilt," as she put it, she hops in the shower as soon as possible and uses a luffa sponge to scrub herself down. During the scouring, she affirms that she is freeing herself of guilt and visualizes it swirling away down the drain to be transmuted into perfect, righteous energy. If she's aware of what they are, she also scrubs off the old roles and beliefs she's held that led to this particular bout of guilt. The pièce de résistance is a rousing rendition of, "I'm gonna wash that guilt right out of myself," which she sings at the top of her lungs.

I've tried Alice's technique and you might want to also. It's fun and lightens up the heaviness guilt can assume.

I let go of guilt effortlessly.

I am a good person even though I make mistakes.

Designing Sacred Space

· ·

BECAUSE A WOMAN IS SO SENSITIVE TO THE nuances of the space around her, her home needs to nourish her soul. We thrive best in a nest that is both a shelter in which to retreat and a launching pad from which to soar.

Each of us has different tastes and needs. What feels sacred to one may jangle another's nerves. We may want our entire house to feel sacred, or a small alter or a modest corner of a garden may suffice perfectly. One of my friends has a private little room chock full of humming-bird symbols where she goes and "breathes a sigh of relief." Another woman's entire home is decorated in vibrant Mexican decor, which soothes her soul; yet another's retreat is a tiny garden under a favorite tree.

In order to figure out how to create sacred space for yourself, take a thoughtful and leisurely stroll through your house and yard. Is there a room, a particular piece of furniture, or a small space that whispers to you, "Welcome home . . . Come, sit here, and relax. Rest, cre-ate, dream, plan, worship . . ."? In space that feels sacred to us, we sigh with relief and soar more effortlessly into our soul selves. We are home. If, on your tour, you find a spot that calls to you, how would you like to augment it? If you don't find a favorite "home" spot, meditate on what it might look like if you did create a sacred space. It will come to you. When we look into our hearts, we know what sort of space nourishes our souls and replenishes our inner resources.

We deserve and *need* for our homes, or special places within them, to reflect our essence. Gift yourself with sacred space.

I give myself permission to create sacred spaces around me.

My home reflects and nourishes my soul.

Intertwining
Soul-Strands

*And remember, we all stumble, every one
of us. That's why it's a comfort to go
hand in hand.*

—E. K. Brough

BEING IN A RELATIONSHIP IS OUR MOST valuable spiritual workshop. Relationships are the threads with which God weaves our earthly world, and the ways we care for and communicate with ourselves and each other create the patterns for our lives.

When we intertwine our soul-strands with others, we are brought face-to-face with our deepest fears and our highest aspirations. We are catapulted to towering heights and dragged to numbing depths, all in the service of soul.

I will admit that, on occasion, I have thought that a simple, solitary spiritual path would be just dandy. Leave me alone, and I'll come home to God wagging—not dragging—my tail behind me. But, in reality, we are relational beings who want and need to be connected to others in meaningful ways, no matter what joys and sorrows are involved. Allowing ourselves to intertwine soul-strands provides us with ample opportunities to love and be loved, and love is the path to Spirit.

Weaving Our Souls Together

. . . .

EACH OF US HAS MUCH TO LEARN FROM relating to others. Because they know us so well, our mates, children, and close friends are often our most resourceful teachers. While this truth may be self-evident, it is frequently difficult at any given moment for us to be good students.

One way to become an eager, or at least a willing, pupil is to realize that we intertwine our soul strands with those of our intimates when we agree to be in relationships. From the weaving together of our individual spirits emerges a much larger picture, that of our soul's work, both individually and jointly.

Keeping that larger soul perspective is vital, especially when things are difficult between us. Remembering our soul connection helps enable us to act from and with love.

To get an image of this joining, sit quietly with your eyes closed and meditate on a relationship between you and a loved one. Allow positive energy to flow from your heart to the other person's. See or imagine your soul-strands rising from the top of your heads. Watch as those beautiful and unique soul-strands weave together, dancing to the music that only your relationship can compose. Delight in the joy of your souls' harmony.

Visualizing like this helps us rise above some of the human issues that often cloud our higher sight, and it allows us to travel into the realm of insight about our soul's commitment of the heart.

I deserve to dance to the music of love.

I weave my heart and soul with those I love.

Making Conscious Connections

. . . .

COMMUNICATION IS AT THE HEART OF OUR
lives and connects our souls with those we love
and with the soul of the world. How we communicate determines whether we build bridges
or create chasms within ourselves, and between
ourselves, others, the environment, and God. If
our communication with ourselves is a contin-
ual crucifixion, our spirits become wounded and
clamp tightly shut. A closed spirit cannot com-
mune with others, soul to soul.

Artful communication, on the other hand,
connects us to ourselves and each other, bonds
us together through strands of energy, actions,
and words. At best, communication becomes a
daily communion, in which we express the highest and deepest within us, and share the very
best of ourselves, thereby calling forth the very
best from others.

We are constantly, intuitively, and innately
communicating. But do we communicate *consciously?* To communicate from our hearts and
souls, we need to commit ourselves to being
aware of how, why, and even when we communicate. Learning to consciously communicate
will help us understand what our intention is

during any particular encounter, especially during times of intense emotion and vulnerability. If our intention is to win, or to be right, we'd better pause until we can change that to a desire for better understanding and connection.

Consciously communicating means that you ask yourself if what you're saying enhances feelings of affinity, safety, and connection in your relationships. If the answer is consistently a yes, you are a valuable teacher and model for supportive relationships, and I am thankful for you. While most of us communicate consciously sometimes, because we are all so vulnerable, we truly need to learn to communicate consciously most, if not all, of the time.

Conscious, artful communication is a sacrament of love, support, and safety that deepens our connections to others.

My goals in communicating are understanding and connection.

I am thoughtful about what I say and do.

Cleansing Your Personal Vase

. . . .

COMMUNICATION IS THE SACRED VESSEL from which we pour the wine of our souls into our lives and relationships. Because of this, we need to clean up any habits that may be tainting the wine. Major poisoning comes from the sludge of self-criticism and chastisement that we often pour on ourselves.

Habitually treating ourselves poorly and severely judging what we do and say causes our spirits to retreat in confusion and fear. In order to express the good, true, and beautiful within us, we must remember to communicate with ourselves gently. It's so important that we speak to ourselves as a dear and cherished friend and are encouraging and supportive within the privacy of our own minds. Doing so helps us evolve into being loving and patient with others as well as ourselves. It is possible to learn to do. I know because I had the dirtiest vessel imaginable when I was younger, and vinegar, not wine, gushed from it onto myself primarily. Most of the whispers of my mind were like daggers in my heart. That's no longer true, and, although changing the pattern was not easy and took commitment and effort, it was well worth the struggle.

In order to break any pattern of verbal self-abuse, we need to be on the lookout for detrimental self-talk and replace it immediately with communication worthy of a soul-friend. To help yourself succeed, close your eyes and invite the image of a vase to come into the theater of your mind. Ask that it symbolize the vessel of communication between you and yourself. Envision your self-talk being poured into this vase. Is it pure and supportive, or clouded and discouraging?

As you are pondering your vase, become aware of the soft sound of water. Looking around, notice a small but beautiful waterfall gently cascading into a crystal pool. Cleanse your vase in it, and, when it is clean, fill it with the wine of your spirit, which pours from the pristine center of your soul.

I am a beloved child of God.
I speak to myself with love and respect.

Awakening the Sleeping Spirit

....

AS HAPPENED TO SLEEPING BEAUTY, A POS-
sessive and jealous fairy (whom I call the world
fairy) can cast her spell on us sometime in childhood, and as we move into the responsibilities
of adulthood, we fall asleep. Doing the "stuff" of
grown-ups, we work, play, raise families, have
friends, and volunteer our services, but all too
often our spiritual connections drift into som-
nolence. Basically, we fall asleep at the wheel
and forget to relate to the soul of ourselves or
our loved ones.

Luckily, we have within us a different kind of
fairy, an intrinsic soul fairy, who communes
with us continuously. She is soft-spoken and
gentle, but persistent. A devoted friend to our
spirits, she whispers inspirations and songs of
love into our ears. We catch hints of her lyrics
and melodies every day, but are often too
sleepy or busy to pay attention. Not to worry,
because her songs are eternal, and she will still
be singing when our thirsty souls convince us to
pay attention.

We can quiet our minds to be able to hear
her songs through meditation. Meditation is listening to the Divine within, and our soul fairy is

a wonderful spokesbeing for the Divine. Let's use her now as an entry through the door of meditation.

With your eyes closed, allow your breath to deepen into a comfortable rhythm. Picture your soul fairy and imagine her giving you a word to use during this meditation. Listen carefully, but without stress or expectation, and allow a word, or short series of words, to float easily into your awareness. Words that often come to me are "Thank You," and "You through me." One friend tenderly says, "Wake up, Spirit." Breathe your words either into your heart center or into your tummy. If your mind wanders off, gently return your attention to your breath and the word or words.

Each time we practice this meditation, we move deeper and deeper into our center, where the Divine sits beside our spirit, which longs to be awakened.

I listen for the songs of my soul fairy.
I invite my spirit to be fully awake.

Listening Deeply

· ·

TO THE SACRED FEMININE VOICE OF OUR hearts, listening is a sacred art. Deeply listening is miraculous for both listener and speaker. When someone welcomes us with open-hearted, accepting, interested listening, our spirits expand and we are inspired to unveil the miracle of our Self.

The Yiddish proverb, "There is no one as deaf as he who will not listen," speaks simply to a basic truth. We have an epidemic of deafness in our world, and the result of not hearing one another in a meaningful way is a profound and poignant loneliness. As plants shrivel without sun and water, we are dying in spirit for lack of deep listening.

The words *heart* and *listen* provide hints about the art of listening deeply. *Heart* contains within it the word *hear*, and *listen* contains the exact same letters as *silent*. In order to hear what is being said and felt, we need to be silent and listen from our hearts; we must close our mouths and give undivided attention to others when they open theirs.

I watched a young mother do this beautifully when her three-year-old son began to continuously interrupt our conversation. She excused herself from me and looked directly in his eyes. "Do you need a little UDA?" she asked. For me, she clarified, "Undivided attention." He said that he did, and this wise mom totally turned her attention to her son, listening deeply. After about five minutes of UDA, he jumped down from the table saying, "Okay, I'm done" and went off to play. Miracle accomplished.

When we practice the sacred art of listening, we intertwine our souls. Deep listening from the heart of the Sacred Feminine fosters understanding, and understanding can miraculously turn into love.

I listen deeply to others.
I listen from my heart.

Letting Love Flow

. . . .

THERE ARE TIMES WHEN OUR COMMITMENT
to our loved ones is more a decision than a feeling. When that is the case, we can allow *agape*,
or the impersonal love of the Divine, to flow
through us to them. Yielding to God's love flowing through, instead of relying on our own abilities to send unconditional regard, is especially
necessary for the times that we do not, on a
human level, give one roaring toot whether this
totally icky other person is loved or not.

When I was angrily sloughing through the
quagmire of my divorce, Annabelle, my spiritual mother and mentor, taught me to sit quietly
with my eyes closed and begin a positive flow
of energy from my heart to another's by imagining the recipient of my energy stream as someone or something that I felt absolutely loving
toward. Often I used one of my children, a
puppy, or a flower.

When the heart flow was solidly established,
very, very slowly I let the picture fade and allowed the image of my former husband to take
its place. If the flow stopped, I would put the
easier recipient back in place and begin the exercise again. I was really doing this more for me

than for him, because I knew that the rage and hate I was experiencing were blocking my ability to open fully to love.

When we block our love to and from another person, we cut off our own energy supply from our spirit-selves. We are short-circuited. As soon as we can restore harmony in ourselves and reactivate our willingness to send unconditional regard (it's perfectly all right if it is *impersonal*), love energy begins to flow back into us from our higher self, and then out to the other person. A closed heart can neither give nor receive, while an open heart is a direct conduit for the Beloved to love through us.

I allow love to flow through me.
I can love even difficult people impersonally.

Neutralizing Knee-Jerks

. . . .

BECAUSE WE ARE HUMAN, WE ALL HAVE knee-jerk reactions—most of which are negative—to certain situations or provocations. But reactions often need to be reviewed or they can shred the dickens out of relationships and our own self-esteem. As the wise Chinese proverb states, "If you are patient in one moment of anger, you will escape a hundred days of sorrow." That's because acting on our knee-jerk responses usually ends up causing us to feel sorrow, guilt, and/or shame. When we go for the jugular, everyone gets bloodied.

Knee-jerk reactions are automatic, out-of-soul responses, and, although we may not stop ourselves from having them, we definitely can stop ourselves from expressing them. Knee-jerks inevitably land on someone else, and disconnection is the result. Separation doesn't draw us closer to each other or to the core of our Selves.

Tricia, a young client of mine, had fractured several relationships with very nice young men because, during emotional encounters, she blurted out whatever came into her mind. Usually, it was hurtful. Being subjected to her venomous strikes eventually caused the men to leave.

After much denial, Tricia finally realized that her wounding, uncontrolled responses were the culprits that kicked the men out of her life. This awareness was the beginning of her ongoing work to neutralize her sabotaging knee-jerk re-actions.

If we are to keep our relationships safe havens for soul-growth and self-expression, we need to neutralize knee-jerks. The old adage of counting to ten is based on pure wisdom.

Today, if something happens to provoke you, pause. Move into your heart. Count if it helps, and excuse yourself for a time-out if you need it. Become aware of your breath. During conflict our breath becomes very shallow. Con-sciously deepen your breathing and ask yourself how you choose to respond. We DO have the choice, and our choices determine whether we connect with others soulfully or experience "a hundred days of sorrow."

I carefully choose my responses.
When upset or confused, I pause and breathe.

Wising Up in the Silence

· ·

WISDOM AND INTUITION ARE BIRTHED IN silence. Before you read on, take a few moments to close your eyes and relax into the hush of silence. Neither asking nor expecting anything of yourself, merely relax into the quietness.

For some of us, it takes practice to feel comfortable with silence, although I believe all of us intuitively understand its value. One of the reasons that it's very important is that only in silence can we hear the feminine energy of our hearts.

If we listen closely in the silence, the Sacred Feminine will show us how to lovingly intertwine soul-strands in our relationships with others and with ourselves. Our relationships can hum with the songs of love only if they are filled with the Sacred Feminine Voice, for she *is* the song of love. She is the harp upon which the strings of compassion and connection quiver. From the Sacred Feminine comes the sweet music composed by living complementary lives with those we love.

"Silence is the language of God; it is also the language of the heart," said Danish statesman and philosopher, Dag Hammarskjöld. The more faithfully we move into the silence, the more attuned we will become to the voice of Spirit.

Today, give yourself the gift of relaxing into the silence. Softly, gently, lovingly allow silence to immerse you in peace. As a result, the music of wisdom and intuition will become clearer and more harmonious.

I relax into the silence today.

I allow the Sacred Feminine to teach me about love.

Communicating Love
Through Action

. . . .

Thought is the blossom,
Language the bud,
Action the fruit behind it.

—R. W. Emerson

IT'S EASY TO SPEAK OF LOVE AND CARING,
but not so easy to match our actions to the
words. The old adage "actions speak louder
than words" is absolutely true because, when we
can be counted on to do as we say we will, trust
is the by-product. Relationships thrive on trust.
In fact, it's best to intimately intertwine our
soul-strands only with those whom we can trust
implicitly. Those are the alliances that will feed
our spirits. Whether a caring relationship is
close or casual, we need to be able to count on
the integrity of ourselves and others.

Being extremely busy when it came time to
move her office, Bonnie told the woman who
owned and operated the moving company to,
"Just pack it and take it to this address." After
a difficult day at another office, Bonnie dragged
herself to the new place, harried, exhausted,

and dreading the thought of unpacking. She opened the door to a sweet surprise—everything was unpacked and arranged *exactly* as it had been in the old office, down to the seashells on the shelves. In the face of such caring by her from-the-heart movers, tears of gratitude flowed, and the remnants of a horrible week seemed to be washed away with them.

Our actions inevitably communicate our true love quotient. What close or casual relationship would benefit from the fruit of action from you? How can you, today, communicate love through action either to yourself or to another?

I match my actions to my words.
I and other people can count on me.

Speaking with Spirit-Tongue

· ·

IN ORDER TO KEEP THE THREADS THAT weave us together from fraying, we need to speak our truth and resolve conflicts within a container of caring. I am able to do this much more consistently when I remember the Four Noble Truths. The wisdom of the four noble truths can be found in many cultures, but I'm sharing knowledge found in The Great Wheel of Life, an ancient circular symbol that has been used by native peoples for thousands of years, and augmented by anthropologist Angeles Arrien and me.

The Four Noble Truths are:

1. SHOW UP and choose to be present to all that life offers. Be a good model—by walking your talk.

2. PAY ATTENTION to what has heart and meaning for you and resonates within your soul.

3. TELL THE TRUTH without blame or judgment. Say what you mean and mean what you say (indigenous peoples call this "speaking with spirit-tongue") or, KEEP NOBLE SILENCE. From an empowered position, choose to remain silent.

4. STAY OPEN, BUT NOT ATTACHED, TO THE OUTCOME. Deeply care, from an objective place. Break old patterns. Practice discernment.

If we did nothing else but adopt and live these four wonderful truths, our spirits would soar to new heights and our relationships would be healthy and holy. Remembering that the bottom line needs to be drawn with love, we can choose to speak with spirit-tongue or maintain noble silence.

I never speak with the intention of hurting.
I honor my truth and speak it caringly.

Enlivening with Enthusiasm

. . . .

ENTHUSIASM COMES FROM THE GREEK *enthousiasmos* and means "having a God within" or "possessed by a divine spirit." I love that! Since our enthusiasm is linked to the God within, to our Divine Spirit, it's incredibly important that we endorse rather than drown fiery excitement.

Many of us have had our enthusiasm dampened as children. Although no one may have purposefully set out to squelch us, it undoubtedly happened, at least on occasion. If we've been silenced, cautioned to "calm down" or, worse yet, put down when enthusiastic, it's even more important for us to tend the fire of enthusiasm within ourselves and others. Doing so will help ignite, or reignite, the divine spark everpresent within our souls.

Close your eyes and allow yourself to sink deeply into the very center of your being. Focus on your breath and encourage it to become slower and deeper. If your mind is chattering, gently turn your attention to your breath and concentrate on drawing it into your heart center. Imagine that it is a little after twilight and you are sitting comfortably in front of a small campfire at the edge of a woods. Over the trees a luminous full moon is rising.

To your delighted surprise, you see a beautiful Being walking down a shaft of moonlight into your circle. With complete candor, you begin to share with this Being your dreams, aspirations, and just-plain-fun ideas She listens with unbounded enthusiasm as she lovingly builds up the campfire as the night becomes cooler. Bask in the warmth of her attention and enthusiasm for your thoughts. Feel yourself becoming inspired and creative as a result.

Today, if only for a few minutes, allow yourself to be possessed by a divinely enthusiastic spirit. Search out at least one thing about which you can unabashedly gush. I bet you'll be surprised how infectious your excitement is to others and how energized you feel as a result.

I am alive with enthusiasm.

I greet my own and others' ideas and inspirations with enthusiasm.

Aligning Our Breath

. . . .

OUR RELATIONSHIPS WITH EACH OTHER
and with ourselves are bound to have some difficult moments. We are all vulnerable human
beings who will, on occasion, have our feelings
hurt. Or we may find ourselves in very painful
situations without a clue regarding how to connect with someone, be helpful to them, or even
cope ourselves.

Since all living things share breath, in difficult times often the best thing we can possibly
do is to breathe together in silence. The following technique helps bring us into alignment
with each other and intertwines our soul-
strands in a very simple, compassionate way.
You can even do it without the other person
knowing it.

Without fuss or bother, gently begin to align
your breath to the breath of the person with
whom you are relating, following his or her
rhythm of inhales and exhales. As you match
him or her, ask the Beloved within you to help
you listen from your heart to any spoken or unspoken message, and then open to hear the still,
small voice of love.

I learned this method from a hospice nurse who worked exclusively with AIDS patients. She said that there were many days when, other than making her patients as comfortable as possible, all she could do was hold them and align her breath with theirs. More often than not, few words were uttered, but there were many tears shed. Tears of all kinds—sadness, frustration, guilt and shame, empathy, compassion, and spiritual joy—overflowed from nurse and patient as she gifted them with her presence and matching breath and they gifted her with their real, and often, luminous feelings.

We can align our breath to augment wonderful feelings as well as assuage troubling ones. Breathe rhythmically with your lover before making love. Duplicate a child's breath as you play together or as they sleep. Be creative and remember that as we align our breath, we align the very soul-strand that is inherent to us all.

*I align my breath with those I want to
connect with deeply.*

My breath connects me to all living beings.

Honoring
Sacred Rights
and Responsibilities

*The true Light is a gentle love
which, rising in you, causes you to look
on the world with understanding and
compassion and respect. When you
respect the souls of your brother and sister, you respect their lives in every way.
This gentle spirit, this respect one for
another, must come. For this is the gener-
ation of the one true Light, and this true
light is that of love.*

—*White Eagle*

THE FEMININE SPIRIT NOURISHES AND gives birth not only to other humans, but ideas and ideals as well. As modern women, we are called to nourish and give birth to the light of gentle love and respect for all people. It is our sacred right and responsibility to realize that we, each and every one of us, is the fulfillment of Divine purpose. Ours are the hearts through which God's love flows; ours are the arms that hold the wounded, weary, and frightened; ours are the voices that can espouse understanding, tolerance, and compassion.

To be equal to the calling of the Spirit within and around us, we need to recognize that we already *are* who we need to be. Of course, as a natural part of our soul's refining process, we all have fears, false beliefs, and wounds to transform. But, beneath the layers of humanity, we are whole. We don't get the holy grail—we are the grail. At our core, we are a cup from which God longs to pour love upon her children. Our sacred mission is to live in a state of love and integrity with ourselves first, and then pour the balm of love and integrity onto our thirsty world.

Living Gently with Yourself and Others

. . . .

AN IRISH PROVERB STATES A SIMPLE TRUTH, "Even a small thorn causes pain." How often, out of thoughtlessness or lack of attention, do we inflict pain, even though we don't want or mean to? We yearn to live gently, and yet gentleness—especially toward ourselves—seems so difficult in our fast-paced lives. When we are frantically trying to abide by a timetable that is at odds with our natural ebb and flow, the ability to breathe deeply and choose our reaction is diminished. Before we know it, a thorny comment is automatically launched.

Lost in the acceleration of our pace is the energy and time for gently supporting and nurturing ourselves and our loved ones. But, with intention, we *can* cultivate the art of gentleness. However, we will need to make a strong commitment to living gently and adopt an *attitude* that supports our resolution. And as usual, we'll need to start this attitude adjustment by treating *ourselves* gently. What a thought!

Of course we expect ourselves to be gentle with others, but aren't we supposed to be our own hardest taskmaster and severest critic? No. In reality, learning to be gentle with ourselves enhances our ability to shine the light of love, trust, and respect on others. Embraced by a nurturing, sensitive *self*, we are better and safer friends and family members. Treating ourselves harshly bruises our hearts, and a bruised heart is more likely to treat others in a bruising way, or at least wish it could.

I believe that we sincerely want to be gentle, but often don't know how. Sometimes all we need to adopt a gentle attitude is some small reminders. What would be a good reminder for you? Maybe a three-by-five card on the refrigerator saying, *Live gently with yourself and others*. Or an agreement with a friend to ask, "Is that gentle?" when you're hard on yourself. Take a few minutes today to give yourself and those you love a soul-enhancing gift—think of ways to welcome the art of gentleness into your life.

I live gently with myself and others.
Without judgment, I remind myself to be gentle.

Transforming Fear

. . . .

MANY OF US FEEL A NEED TO CLIMB OUT OF the black holes of fear into which we have been pushed or have leapt of our own accord—never to be afraid again. It's unreasonable to expect that we can evolve to a point where we never experience fear, but it is perfectly reasonable to believe that we can free ourselves from the limitations fear imposes, so that it neither dictates how we live nor totally distracts us from our spiritual path.

We are born with only two natural fears— fear of falling and fear of loud noises. All other fears are learned. If we learned them, we can *un*learn them. And unlearn them we must, for fear blocks out love and love is the vehicle for Spirit. That's why, as our fear is transformed, we are able to access more of our soul-spark, which is powerfully gentle, strong, and wise. Feminine qualities are desperately needed to create a safe and harmonious world.

Wanda, a client of mine, was so fearful that she couldn't leave her house to come to my office. So, for a short while, I went to her. With great effort and courage, Wanda began to track down the fearful beliefs buried within her psyche. Her most debilitating fear came from being the only daughter in a family of three brothers. As a product of the boys-are-better society, Wanda's mother unwittingly led her to believe that she wasn't as good as her brothers and could never do anything right.

Haunted by the fear that she actually had no right to exist, Wanda increasingly limited her life until she *wasn't* really living. Becoming aware of the fears she'd learned at (and sometimes over) her mother's knee, Wanda began to disentangle herself from them through therapy and dedicated work. The day she finally walked through my office door was one of celebration.

Like Wanda, there are times when we can't do it alone. If you feel at a loss, please be gentle with yourself and seek help. Fear, transformed, translates into empowerment and love. GREAT!

I have the wisdom to seek help.

I have the courage to unlearn fears.

Evolving into Simplicity

. . . .

HUMAN CONSCIOUSNESS IS EVER-EVOLVING.
Actually *everything* is always evolving, and, interestingly, evolution is not toward more com-
plexity as we might suspect but toward *simplicity*.
That is why our souls thirst for simplicity; in
their wisdom, they know that love and spirit are
simple.

While talking to Debra, a recently widowed
friend, I was struck by her answer to my question, "Were the last few weeks of Todd's illness
very difficult for your family?" Surprisingly, she
answered, "No. By then we all knew that he
would die, and we lived moment-to-moment.
Our life was trimmed down to the simplest
things—a tiny smile, a drink of water, flashes of
deep heart connection through feeling or even
a little talking. It was the simplest and the *sweet-
est* time of my life." Wow!

Debra's comments resonated with an almost
wordless thirst within me. Simplicity. Sweet-
ness. Time for reflection and relating. Umm . . .
The upshot of that conversation is a deep commitment on my part to trim the unnecessary
and the unwanted from my life without there
having to be a crisis to provoke it, and to get

progressively better at discerning when less is more. Sort of a continous soul garage sale.

Right now, gently, and with great compassion, take a deep breath and look at your calendar for the next week. If it is more crowded than you feel comfortable with, ponder what activities and obligations may be unnecessary or unwanted. Without judgment, ask yourself if you are an "automatic yes'er." Do you say yes even if you feel no?"

Are you thirsty for the solace of simplicity? If so, tuck in your heart and mind a promise to evolve into more simplicity. Start by eliminating just one tiny or tremendous thing that feels unnecessary or unwanted. Simplicity can be simply and soulfully wonderful.

Simple is as simple doesn't.

I am creating a simple and sweet lifestyle that is right for me.

Balancing on the Cusp

....

WE ARE ON THE BRINK OF A SPIRITUAL
renaissance in our post-industrial world, poised
on the cusp of a new paradigm that has endless
possibilities for new beginnings. In ever-grow-
ing numbers, we are becoming aware of an ancient, mysterious, spiritual reality of oneness.
This mystery was never mysterious to mystics
and indigenous peoples who intuitively lived
with the awareness that we are all linked together—people, plants, and animals—as creations of the Divine.

In our culture, however, we have been satu-
rated with the almost universal belief in *separateness*, not oneness, which is why it is sometimes
hard for us to see how we are related. It's true
that we look separate, but if we could see the
energy fields within and emanating from us, we
would see that our energy intermingles with all
energies: trees, teenagers, Tasmanians, tantrum
throwing tots. Everyone, everything.

It's an awesome idea, isn't it? It can also be a
scary idea if our security rests in being separate
and/or superior, or in being *sure* of the rules and
realities. Nonetheless, energetic oneness is an

actuality discovered by scientific research and backed up by the new laws of quantum physics.

Like most of us, I'm teetering on the cusp of the new paradigm, and, although I believe in the concept of oneness, I neither *know* it nor *experience* it on a regular basis. One technique I use to help myself move beyond the belief in separateness is visualizing my energy dancing and mingling with both animate and inanimate others, like energy soup. I also remind myself when I meet people going through my day, "I and this person are one" like Christ said of he and his father. I'm not sure how much progress I'm making, but I do feel more tolerant and connected much of the time. I'm going to keep trying, because oneness is the essence of spiritual love.

I and my sister and brother are one.

Love is essence.

Practicing Beginner's Mind

. . . .

I FIND THE BUDDHIST CONCEPT OF BEGIN-
ner's mind incredibly refreshing. As adults,
we've spent so much time and energy filling
our minds with information that they begin to
resemble cluttered attics, so glutted with stuff
that we can hardly move through them, let
alone find what we're looking for. The idea of
beginner's mind is to empty, not fill, in order
to be ready for anything and open to everything. It's about going back to a time where
we knew nothing and therefore took nothing
for granted.

It's actually very relaxing to practice beginner's mind. For example, before I was to give
a talk to a large group that had labeled me an
"expert on relationships," I was anxiety-ridden
to the point of sleeplessness. To make matters
worse, the "expert" and her husband were not
on the best of terms right then. (Don't you hate
it when that happens?) I was afraid I wouldn't
remember all that I knew, that somehow the
audience would know that Gene and I were in a
hard place, and that I would embarrass myself,
my hosts, and the planet. You know, the usual.

Thankfully, just before I was supposed to leave for the talk, I ran across a quote by Suzuki Roshi that said, "In the beginner's mind there are many possibilities; in the expert's mind there are few." Quick as a wink I dropped the "expert" label and gave the talk as a sister pilgrim on the sometimes rocky path of relationships. My relaxed attitude seemed to translate to the audience because we had a great time.

Anxiety slams the door shut on our mind's attic, whereas beginner's mind not only keeps our attic door open, but opens the door to the attic of intuition, which is a vast storehouse of wisdom and joy.

Just for the fun of it, put the book down and look at your surroundings with new eyes. Really see the objects or vistas. Explore your space with the openness of a curious child. Fill yourself with the wonder of beginner's mind.

I practice the art of beginner's mind.

I am open to many possibilities.

Taking the Helm

. . . .

SPIRITUAL GROWTH LIES BEYOND BLAME, for blame casts out love and keeps us locked in the childish victimized action of finger pointing. That's why our spirits and souls remain immobile, undeveloped, and thwarted in direct proportion to the amount of blame we harbor.

Since chronic, congealed blame dwarfs and deforms our spiritual development, one of our major life-tasks is to heal, transform, and let go of any blaming energy that we harbor toward ourselves or others. Dropping blame means not *assigning* responsibility to others for our lives, feelings, actions, and words but *assuming* it ourselves.

By taking responsibility, I'm talking about choosing how we *respond* in all situations, and assessing our part in creating them or allowing them to happen. I am *not* talking about blaming ourselves by thinking something like, "I have cancer. What horrible thing have I done to deserve this?" But rather, "I have cancer. What emotions or lifestyle choices may have created a vulnerability to it, and what can I do now to change that? How can this situation polish my spirit?"

I believe that we're not helpless in the face of a random world, but that in some unfathomable way our souls have agreed to learn lessons provided by many of the circumstances we face. Assuming responsibility frees us by putting us at the helm of our lives, in charge of mapping out the routes to take on our physical and spiritual journey.

I was talking to Laurel, a wonderfully wise young woman, about the concept of taking responsibility even in difficult situations, and she said something I'll never forget. "Well," she chuckled, "the way I look at it is that, in the In-Between-Lives Lounge, I went to the registration table and said, 'I'll take everything you've got!' So, I'm going to learn from it."

We can lovingly take the helm of our lives, chart our own course, and learn from even treacherous waters. Gently ask yourself if you are sailing in uncharted waters right now. If so, what might you learn by taking the helm and turning in a new direction?

All situations can polish my spirit.
I take responsibility—not blame—for my life.

Caring for Grandmother Earth

. . . .

*To indigenous people, Earth is a living being.
Among the Lakota we call Earth our grandmother, and you do not rape your grandmother.
Because she is the mother of all living beings,
you are related to everything that lives—
every blade of grass, every pine needle, every
grain of sand. Even the rocks have life. Since
you rely on all this life for your sustenance,
you have to be respectful.*

—Russell Means, Arapaho Activist

AS WOMEN OF SPIRIT, ONE OF THE MOST
urgent responsibilities we have is to become respectful citizens of Grandmother Earth, not
merely consumers or conquerors, and to teach
others to do the same. Grandmother Earth is
our sustainer and inspiration. She not only provides a home and sustenance, but her measure-
less beauty opens a thousand windows to show
us God. Her vast mountains remind us of the
endless peaks of our own courage, the fathom-
less depths of her seas reflect our own enigmatic
and unplumbed treasures, and the endless span
of her ever-changing sky invites our spirits to

soar on the wings of eagles. Next to life itself, Grandmother Earth is God's most precious gift, and it is our sacred responsibility to cherish her so that our beloved children will inherit her riches.

Today, in reality or in your mind's eye, go to a place on the breast of Grandmother Earth where you feel her power and are inspired by her beauty. Make yourself comfortable and invite the wonder of her priceless and countless gifts to permeate your heart and soul. Ask her what she desires from and of you. Listen for her voice in the wind and from the depths of your heart.

I love and respect Grandmother Earth.

I nourish the earth as she nourishes me.

Slowing the Merry-Go-Round

. . . .

IF YOUR LIFE NO LONGER FEELS MERRY BUT, in fact, seems more like a perpetual "harried-go-round," then perhaps you are out of sync with the cycles of nature, which are leisurely and rather slow. Sister Moon uses a full month to wax and wane. Flowers bud and bloom slowly. Babies take nine months to fully develop, and we spend an entire lifetime maturing and growing old. But we, goaded by unreasonable internal and external demands, regularly speed our merry-go-round up until it's hard to hang on to our good humor, let alone fill up our spirits.

To have the energy for spiritual growth, we have a sacred responsibility to discern how fast we want our merry-go-round to go. Of course the desired pace will change periodically depending on circumstances, and that is great as long as we have a choice about the velocity of our lives. There will be times when we want to walk in the race of life rather than run. It's easier on our knees, it allows us to see the scenery, and it leaves us enough breath to talk to a friend and enough quiet to hear our own intuitive wisdom. At other times, an all out run may be exhilarating and will invigorate our hearts, souls, and minds. It's our choice. We just have to make sure that we are choosing our own pace.

With your eyes gently closed, invite the image of a carousel to appear in your mind. Leisurely climb aboard and feel it as it begins to move. How do you like this merry-go-round? Is it circling at a speed that is comfortable for you? Do you like the horse you are on? Is the seat comfortable?

You are the director of your visual picture. Create the ideal carousel, traveling at a satisfactory speed, and then decide how you might want to re-create that rhythm in your day.

I choose the pace that is right for me today.

I match my life to my unique rhythm.

Actualizing Our Vision

. . . .

NO MATTER WHAT OUR LIFE HAS BEEN LIKE up to this point, it is never too late to be who we are meant to be. Each of us arrives in this life with special talents, aptitudes, and dreams, which we add to, augment, and refine as we mature. These aspirations and yearnings are the visions of our souls, the blueprints of our very being. It is our sacred assignment to actualize our personal visions as best we can, both for our own fulfillment, and as gifts to the planet and humankind. If we sacrifice our dreams or denigrate our gifts out of fear or as a concession to others' desires, we set ourselves up for a life of disappointment and resentment.

Noted scholar, Joseph Campbell, summed up the consequences of giving up our vision succinctly when he said, *"Hell is living someone else's life."* When I first heard that, I was in hell, having given up all my dreams and turning myself inside out in hopes of saving my first marriage. It didn't work.

Although living someone else's life and burning our own dreams and talents on the pyres of fear or obligation may sometimes appear to be succeeding, it never does on the soul level. At the level of Essence, we are being called to be a unique prism through which the Divine can be reflected. In response, every fiber of our being is magnetically drawn toward becoming who we were meant to be. Anything less is hell for our spirit.

Living our own life does not make us selfish and self-centered. Quite the contrary. When we actualize our vision, we become *centered* in our hearts and connected to our spirits, which naturally makes us more loving and less selfish.

What are your special gifts and talents? Do you feel comfortable about how you are expressing them? If so, great. If not, what one small step can you take today or tomorrow to actualize your unique vision?

*Each day I become more aware of my vision
for myself and my life.*

I deserve to live my own life.

Making Peace with Risk

. . . .

RISK IS A FOUR-LETTER WORD. BUT THEN, so are live, life, love, and easy. Almost everything has an element of risk involved, and it's perfectly natural to be wary of risk. It's even okay to be terrified occasionally, but terror needs to be accepted as something to *work through*, not used as a stop sign.

If fear of risk does stop you from living the way you would like, please find help through therapy or a support group. There are times when we need someone else to hold the light for us while we venture into the dark cellars of our subconscious to ferret out fear.

A therapist friend of mine took the risk of seeing very disturbed clients and, when one committed suicide, every therapist's nightmare came true—the family sued her. The "justice" system activated every shred of fear she had cowering in her cellar, so she escaped to the beach to try and pull herself together. The shark's teeth sprinkled along the water's edge gave my friend an idea. At all subsequent court hearings she carried shark's teeth in her pocket. Fingering them while in the presence of the attorneys helped remind her that she, too, carried some shark energy and could keep herself safe by not being intimidated by the court process and by setting acceptable parameters for herself. It was difficult to make peace with the risks of private practice, but she continued working and is a much stronger person because of the experience.

In order to really expand our spiritual wings, we need to make peace with risk, transform fear, and create a deep sense of security within our hearts. A helpful gift we can give others as we go through our own process is to pray that our efforts are for them as well as ourselves. Asking that our work reach out to benefit the world gives us a sense of purpose and may even level out bumpy roads for others in ways we can't comprehend.

I accept risk as a part of life.
I keep myself as safe and secure as I can.

Gathering in Circles

. . . .

WOMEN EVERYWHERE ARE GATHERING AT THE
spring-fed wells of Spirit to share their hearts
and join hands as they move toward more completely expressing their boundless love, magnificent wisdom, and compassionate intuition. To
these limitless wells, each of us carries her *own*
container. Each of us fills her *own* jar. And, each
of us is also called to walk with her sisters along
the way providing support, guidance, encouragement, inspiration, and love.

The best we have to give is ourselves. Each
time we gather in a sisterly circle that calls forth
our best, a new pattern is stitched into the fabric of the Spirit-quilt that we are fashioning together, and we are warmed and protected in its
folds. One women's group I know of that has
met together for three years is committed to
completing what they called their "no more
guilt quilt." Collectively and individually they
help each other get the guilt-monkey off their
backs.

Do you have a circle of women who cherish
your hopes, are kind to your dreams, and recognize your uniqueness? Is there a safe place where
your spirit is ennobled and you see yourself re-

flected in the eyes of love and acceptance? It doesn't matter whether your circle is small or vast. The important thing is that you are lovingly valued no matter how you feel or what you do, and also that you feel gently challenged to grow your soul. If you don't currently have such a circle, I encourage you to create one.

An ennobling and comforting circle is also as near as your wise imagination. Close your eyes and allow yourself to effortlessly drift into a relaxed state. Visualize yourself surrounded by others who care deeply for you. Sink into their collective arms and accept the love and appreciation they offer. When you're ready, allow love to flow from you to them until you are an integral part of the circle, giving and receiving equally.

I surround myself with people who care for me.

I am safe in a circle of loving friends.

Flowing Through,
Not Damming Up

IN THE HOLY LAND, THE JORDAN RIVER IS
the source for two lakes. In one, fish are plenti-
ful, wildlife roams its beautiful shores, and thriv-
ing villages line its verdant coastline as waters
flow through the Lake of Galilee blessing animals, crops, and people alike. Although a recipient of the same in-flow from the Jordan River,
the Dead Sea is just that—desolate, deserted.
No good for anyone or anything.

The only difference between the two lakes is
that one gives, and the other does not. The
Lake of Galilee has both an entrance and an
outlet allowing the source to flow *through* it,
while the Dead Sea receives the waters of the
river but doesn't allow them to leave. As a result
of hoarding the blessings it receives, the Dead
Sea became stagnant and lifeless.

Hearing the above analogy in a sermon,
Ann, a client of mine suffering from depression,
honestly evaluated where she was on the Dead
Sea–Lake of Galilee continuum. Depressed and
yet excited by her discovery, she realized that

she was like the Dead Sea in terms of giving to others.

Much to her chagrin (and to her credit, I thought), she acknowledged how much she focused on herself and how narrow her world had become. Courageously, she made a decision to volunteer at a local hospital one day a month. At first, it was only her commitment and a picture of the Dead Sea on her refrigerator that got her out of the house and to the hospital. Eventually, she was volunteering one day a week and looking forward to it. Not surprisingly, having become a blessing to others, she was blessed with a significant lessening of her depression.

The Source, by whatever name you call it, longs to flow into us as a blessing and *through* us as a stream of living water, blessing others. God loves to use us as a floodgate for good. Are you dammed up? Do the waters of love flow through you? Make a promise to yourself today to become like the Lake of Galilee.

I invite divine energy to flow through me.

I enjoy giving to others.

Creating
Spiritual
Touchstones

*The best and most beautiful things in the
world cannot be seen or even touched.
They must be felt with the heart.*

—Helen Keller

I AGREE WITH HELEN KELLER'S IDEA THAT the best and most beautiful things in the world must be felt with the heart. We can help wonder and beauty permeate our souls by surrounding ourselves with spiritual touchstones that gently nudge our hearts toward remembering the good, true, and beautiful within us and our lives. Remembering feeds our souls.

More often than not, spiritual touchstones are very personal, triggering private memories and beliefs. Cherished objects, rituals, attitudes, habits, and places that center us in our hearts, bring us solace, and help us remember that we are not alone can all be considered spiritual touchstones. A spiritual touchstone may be as momentous as an elaborate wedding ceremony or as simple as the way we greet the day; they may be as valuable as a priceless heirloom or as unpretentious as an acorn. Incorporated into our daily lives, such touchstones can prompt us to be more loving, promote peace of mind, inspire us to a higher purpose, and remind us that we are spiritual beings.

Blessing with Ritual

. . . .

RITUALS SPEAK THE LANGUAGE OF THE SOUL.
During meaningful ritual, divine energy is absorbed not only by our brains but in our hearts
and souls as well. Creating and taking part in a
ceremony, whether a tiny, solitary blessing or a
grand pageant, opens our hearts, connects us
with our community and makes us more accessible to ourselves, others, and God.

Profoundly valuable are blessing ceremonies.
In them, we intentionally sprinkle Divine grace
upon the blessed. Blessing someone or something lifts it into the care and light of God. As
we bless, our spirits are also lifted.

Our daily existence is under-blessed; nothing is too minuscule or too magnificent not to
benefit from being blessed. We can bless the ill
and weary, the food we eat, dead animals along
the road, our faces—wrinkles and all—and wartorn countries and the children suffering in
them. We can bless anything, even—perhaps,
especially—our government and political parties.
Blessings can be very simple—a silent inward
bow, an outstretched hand, the murmuring of a
few heartfelt words, a few minutes of deep listening, a sincere thank you. As we bless, we

offer our good wishes and make ourselves a conduit for Spirit to flow through.

One of the most moving ceremonies for me was when our family gathered to bless our grandson before he was born. Each of us, in our own way, blessed the forming baby, the mother and her health, and both the mom and dad for the role they were willingly assuming. We told his spirit how much we looked forward to his arrival. After the blessing, our daughter shared that she felt much better, encouraged by our support, and more peaceful about the baby's well-being.

All blessing rituals—private or public—are powerful touchstones that call forth God's love to sanctify both recipient and sender. Take the opportunity today to look through the eyes of Spirit and bestow one or two silent blessings onto people or circumstances that come into your life.

God flows through me as a blessing to myself and others.

God is blessing me now.

Acknowledging Our Abilities

· ·

PROUD OF COMPLETING GRADUATE SCHOOL and finding a good job in her field, Angela recently congratulated herself by buying a small diamond ring to complement her wedding ring. Having been a dedicated stay-at-home mom until now, gifting herself with something as significant as a ring was unusual for Angela, but it felt right that she did it.

The diamond became a literal touchstone for Angela. When feeling stressed, inadequate, at odds with a loved one, or in need of a boost, she developed a private little ritual that restores her equilibrium: She wears the diamond solitaire alone, without her wedding ring. The facets in it symbolize the many aspects of her being, she told me, and the rainbows of light sparkling from it help her remember that she sees loving and reflecting the light of God as her highest purpose. And, very importantly, the single diamond reminds her of her strength and inspires her to feel good about who she is and all that she's accomplished. Smiling, she said, "It just sits there on my finger saying, 'You're good, and you have good to give, so relax.'"

Gently close your eyes for a minute and mentally wander through your mementos. Enjoy them. Allow them to transport you back in time and space by the memories they evoke. Is there one that especially symbolizes your unique abilities, talents, and/or gifts? If so, ask your wise subconscious to help you uncover a way that this object can remind you of your special excellence. This is your personal ritual, so nothing is too silly or grandiose. If the right symbol was not available in your mementos, gift yourself with one when you find it.

Spiritual touchstones that help us acknowledge our abilities help to amplify them, thereby allowing us to spread more good to ourselves, others, and Mother Earth, who needs all the good she can get. Actually, we all do!

I am good, and I have good to give.
I am capable, strong, and courageous.

Touching to Remember

. . . .

WE ARE SENSUOUS BEINGS. WHILE OUR SENSE of touch brings us much pleasure, it's also essential for our emotional well-being. Motherless baby monkeys choose to cuddle with a towel-wrapped wire figure rather than stay around an unwrapped one even though the uncovered "mom" has food by her. We humans are no different than the little monkeys; we need tactile stimulation and solace.

A friend of mine is waging a herculean battle against the cancer invading many areas of her body. Accompanying her to each procedure and all hospital stays is a stuffed lamb given to her by a woman mentor. Gerrie feels less alone and derives physical and emotional comfort from holding her lamb or having him where she can see him. At first, she said it seemed weird to be a grown woman carrying a rather large stuffed toy, but she became increasingly comfortable as doctors, nurses, and friends accepted the lamb as a natural part of her healing.

But the lamb is *not* just a toy for Gerrie, who sees him as a symbol for Christ, the Lamb of God. I wouldn't be surprised if Christ didn't embody that little toy lamb on occasion in order to comfort his pain-ridden child.

As sensual beings, we need touchstones around us that we can feel in order to nourish our souls and warm our hearts. Such symbols frequently become poignant reminders that we are not alone, but are precious and invaluable, lovable and forever loved by the Divine. As we touch items infused with meaning for us, we can more easily feel ourselves held in the ever-lasting arms of the Beloved—nurtured, cherished, and comforted.

What touches your heart when you see or feel it? What objects have you gathered around yourself that nourish your soul? We all have them, but oftentimes don't remember to let them soothe us. Just for fun, put one of your symbols in a prominent place as a reminder that you are loved and valued.

I am comforted by meaningful symbols.
I am a loved and lovable child of the Divine.

Swimming in Miracles

· ·

EACH DAY WE HAVE THE CHOICE TO SEE
what happens as miraculous or ho-hum, and
how we choose, dramatically affects our perception of life. The other day miracles were
flopping around my feet like little silver
grunions at the water's edge. The biggest one
happened as I was alone, stewing about how to
get home after my bike was sabotaged in a
semi-remote area. Just before I dissolved into
frustrated tears, a young man happened by who
had the strength and know-how to fix my bike.
He was only the second person I'd seen all
morning.

Being miracle-primed by my knight in shiny
bike clothes, I began noticing miracles everywhere. They included a great idea jumping
from my heart to the computer screen, totally
bypassing my mind, and the top to the teriyaki
sauce landing gooey side up when I dropped it.

I started thinking about the reality that, even
though we may be blind to them, miracles are
always swimming around us and are made visible by perceiving life through a lens of wonder
and awe. Viewing tiny incidents, synchronici-
ties, and coincidences as minor miracles creates

an aura of the miraculous, which lifts our hearts. Henry David Thoreau encouraged us to, "Associate reverently and as much as you can, with your loftiest thoughts." Being miracle-minded invites us into reverence.

Seeing is *creating*. It seems that the more we recognize even the smallest miracle, the more there are to see. When our hearts are tuned to-ward perceiving miracles, we draw more to us. It's as if the Miracle Makers spread the word, "Hey, everybody! She's finally noticing and ap-preciating what we've been doing. Let's give 'er a good dousing!"

Swimming in miracles puts us in the flow and allows us to feel the waves of gentle kisses bestowed upon us by a benevolent universe. Create some miracles in your life today by *seeing* the ones that are already joyfully swimming around you.

I notice and celebrate even the tiniest miracle.

*My heart is deeply grateful
for the miracles sprinkling my days.*

Greeting Each Newborn Day

. . . .

WAKING UP IS THE FIRST GIFT THAT WE receive each day. With it, comes the opportunity to set the tone for all of our waking hours. If we usually lament, "Oh, God! It's morning . . ." we can make a big difference in our attitude and energy level by simply changing our greeting to something like, "Thank you, God, for letting me see this morning." When we approach life in this manner, we connect to the wonder of being alive and remember our relationship to the Divine.

If you're already a "lark" instead of a "night owl" and spring out of bed fully awake and enthusiastic, then the following meditation isn't for you, but you may want to read it just to congratulate yourself on mornings well done.

Softly close your eyes and begin to breathe deeply, in through your nose and out through your mouth. As you inhale invite relaxation to flow into your entire body, especially into your brain. Melt into the warmth and comfort of a relaxed body and mind. Absorb the sensation. Compassionately and impersonally, remember how you normally wake up. Without judgment, ask yourself if you are entirely happy with the way you usually greet the day.

If the answer is no, imagine how you'd like to change your greeting. For instance, what would it be like if you decided to greet each new day with a welcoming smile, just as you would greet a returning old friend? In terms of perspective and language, how could you choose to befriend each virgin day? Slowly, gently visualize yourself in bed right before waking. See yourself, in the perfect, right time and way, awakening to the gift of a pure, new day. Greet it in the fresh way that you imagined. How does that feel?

We create a powerful connection to Spirit by greeting each newborn day with enthusiasm and thankfulness.

This day is a gift from the Divine and I rejoice in it.

When the face in the mirror frowns, I smile back.

Enjoying Several Seconds
of Bliss

. . . .

ALTHOUGH WE MAY HAVE EXTENDED PERIODS
of profound joy, most of our truly blissful moments are fleeting. Like sexual orgasms, they are
short, but sweetly change us physically, emotionally, and spiritually. We need to gather
these blissful moments as we would precious
gems and thread them on a memory strand to be
lovingly caressed and reverently remembered
with gratitude. When used like prayer beads,
each memory creates several seconds of bliss for
our souls and a rendezvous with the Divine.

Seconds that bathe my spirit in bliss include
a short conversation in which I feel deeply understood, a beautiful fox in the driveway, receiving unexpected appreciation from my
children, seeing a picture that reminds me of
living in Hawaii, being gleefully greeted by my
grandson, and a minute in meditation when I
feel wholly connected with the Beloved.

Take a little quiet time to think of, or write
down, some of *your* blissful moments. When
you have a list compiled, gently close your eyes
and allow yourself to move into a calm, relaxed

state. Settle down comfortably and imagine yourself transported to a fabulous room filled with every conceivable precious and semi-precious gem. In this magical space there are also other treasures that fill your heart with a deep appreciation for their unique qualities.

Leisurely wander among the riches. Choose a strand of some fine, yet strong, material upon which to string your blissful moments. With great care, pick an appropriate symbol for each memory and add it to your strand in exactly the way that pleases you. After you have completed your strand, find a cozy spot where you feel snug and content. With a prayerful attitude caress the touchstones upon your strand. Take the memory of each blissful moment into your heart and feed your soul with its exquisite loveliness. Before returning from this meditative prayer, decide on a place in your home or on your person where you would like your memory strand to abide.

I am thankful for the moments of bliss that bless my life.

I stop often to enjoy several seconds of bliss.

Lifting into the Light

. . . .

WHILE RELIGION AND MYSTICISM HAVE LONG recognized the power of prayer to affect our energy, attitude, and healing, science is now hopping on the bandwagon. My favorite scientific study was done at Spindrift Institute, where grass seeds were soaked in salt water to keep them from germinating. The seeds were then divided into three groups. The first group was left alone. The second was prayed for by volunteers using directed prayer such as, "Please help these seeds to germinate." The third was the recipient of nondirected prayer that included such statements as, "Thy will be done," or visualizing the seeds whole and perfect and able to germinate if it is the right outworking for them in God's eyes.

Interestingly, none of the seeds from the first group sprouted. And, although some of the ones in the directed prayer group did germinate, *two to four* times as many seeds sprouted when they were prayed for in a nondirective way.

After reading about this study, I decided to place a perpetual prayer candle on my kitchen counter. Beside the candle is a little box in which I place the names of people for whom I want to pray. Before lighting a new candle, I put my hands around it and pray some version of the following: "Mother/Father God, please infuse this candle with your energy so that each person here will feel the touch of your blessing, the kiss of your compassion, and the solace of your arms." For me, the candle acts as a reminder to lift those named into the light of God for the perfect, right outworking in His/Her eyes.

Our prayers are important and valuable, but it appears that, for the best outcome of all souls concerned, the more nondirective we can be, the better. Realizing how valuable they are, what prayers can you offer today, for yourself and others?

I trust that the Divine and her angels know best.

I lift myself and others into the light of God.

Receiving Solace from the Moon

· ·

IN PLAIN VIEW, SHE READILY DISPLAYS HER cycles of illumination and shadow, which are powerful enough to influence vast oceans. Steady, constant, incredibly beautiful, she brings light into the darkness. The moon is our icon, eternally feminine—a celestial mentor, infusing us with the recognition of our own oftentimes shadowy brilliance.

Throughout the centuries, as religions espoused the idea that only the masculine was holy, the power and significance of Sister Moon was progressively downgraded. But a more balanced awareness is emerging and we are realizing that to be whole, holiness must naturally embrace all complementary aspects of being— masculine and feminine, darkness and light, body and spirit, thought and feeling.

As women, we carry the essence of femininity that is symbolized by Sister Moon within the cells of our bodies and the fabric of our souls. Intuitively we can recognize the significance of Luna, the Creator Goddess, and we can invite her to resume her rightful place as our teacher. Once revered and called by the sacred names of "Mother of the Universe," "the

Old Woman Who Never Dies," and "The Eternal One," the moon can bring us solace while inspiring us to learn from and respect all of our own natural cycles—the ebbs and flows, ups and downs, and the waxing and waning.

One night after putting her children to bed Judy, a young woman going through a painful divorce, sat on the floor and leaned her forehead on the sliding glass door weeping uncontrollably. As her tears slowed, she felt as if she were being cradled by a loving and tender grandmother. Resting in those gentle arms, a little glimmer of peace began to shine in her heart. "When I opened my eyes, the first thing I saw was the full moon, and I just seemed to know that hers were the arms that held me. Ever since then I've felt a very special kinship with the moon."

As daughters of the moon we, too, are called to bring light into darkness. What tears can you dry today? What gentle arms can you provide for yourself or another?

Waxing and waning
Bringing light into darkness
She smiles her blessing.

Sending Love Darts

. . . .

LOVE IS THE SOURCE; FROM IT FLOWS OPEN-hearted trust, service, honor, awe, humor, compassion, commitment, and pristine joy. This sounds esoteric and highfalutin', but it's simply a matter of energy. We all know how energized we feel when love is flowing freely in our lives and, in contrast, how stymied we feel when love is frozen. Why? Because, when love is freely flowing, we are in tune with the energy of our soul-self. When love is blocked we are cut off from it.

The ultimate gift of all relationships is energy—an exorbitant, lavish, luxurious profusion of energy. When flowing, such energy is a creative fountain, a font of well-being from which we cannot only revitalize ourselves and others, but tackle projects that serve the greater whole.

When we're "in the flow" with God, ourselves, and others, we are energized and have incredible stamina. But if our love-flow is sidetracked or stymied, we feel droopy, cut off, and out of steam. So how do we keep the flow going? One of the simplest and most effective ways is to consciously send little love darts from our hearts toward people we encounter throughout the day—especially the irritating ones.

Love darts are quick, silent blessings to the recipient—something like, may you be peaceful and happy—and little reminders to ourselves that keep our hearts warm, moist, and fertile. Try it with people whom you're crazy about, and those with whom you have difficulty.

My favorite target is a surly check-out person at the grocery store. I don't know how he feels being pricked by a love dart, but I certainly feel better after sending one than I do when I grouse to myself about how rude he is.

Our commitment to living from the heart and sending positive regard infuses us with the energy of love, and there is no greater or more efficient fuel. Send a quiver of love darts today.

I bless myself with lots of little love darts.

The love of God flows through my heart,
blessing all those whom I encounter.

Being Sensitive
to God's Bouquets

IF WE OPEN THE DOOR TO OUR HEART, God will throw in a bunch of flowers. Because these sweet bouquets come in myriad forms and are often very subtle, we need to be sensitive to their presence. Learning to open up to receive God's flowers is so important, for they can ease our hearts and become precious reminders of Her caring and concern for us.

God's bouquets often come to us when we need them most, and being able to perceive them is a talent we can cultivate through awareness. Paradoxically, we have a tendency to be very inner-focused and less aware of externals when we are in some sort of pain, so the first step toward seeing God-signs is to actively look for them.

Not long ago I was in the painful place of questioning the meaning and message of my work concerning activating heart energy in relationships. I was still in the loss-of-confidence and lamenting stage, when I found a piece of marble at a sculpting studio—a heart half emerging from a cool white square. A blunt but valuable bouquet from God, and I got the message. Although in need of filing and smoothing, just as my own heart is, the half heart sits on my desk as a reminder to be wholehearted in my commitment to my work no matter what the consequences or rewards.

Since then, I have stumbled on two more rocks that look like fully formed hearts and a cattail in the form of a heart. The last rock, which had *two* hearts on it, made me laugh in acknowledgment, "Thank you for the vote of confidence! I can sit back down at my computer now."

God's bouquets surround us, but we must be sensitive to their presence in order to enjoy and benefit from them. Give yourself the gift of being on the lookout, for you never know when the heavenly FTD will drop a gift from God into your heart.

I open my eyes to God's blessings.

I am surrounded by reassurance from the Divine.

Cleansing Keepsakes

....

INTUITIVELY WE KNOW THAT OBJECTS CARRY the energy of those who have owned them. Most of us like to have at least a few keepsakes around us precisely because we can *feel* their energy, which is excellent as long as it is positive. Because they are such storehouses of energy, it's best to keep objects or pictures that carry only positive energy and memories. However, if there is something that you want to keep, but it feels negative to you or brings up painful memories, it can be cleansed and neutralized through prayer and ritual.

Elizabeth was given diaries kept by her grandmother and great-grandmother, neither of whom were grand. Although she wanted to keep the diaries because of their historical significance, Elizabeth felt uncomfortable with them in her home. We created a cleansing ritual for her to do after which she could assess how the books felt to her. First, Elizabeth gave thanks for both women and asked that they be healed and blessed. She then asked Mother Mary to cleanse the diaries, transforming and transmuting the energy in them to energy compatible with the mind of Christ. She evoked her guardian angels to take any stubborn negative energy out of the books and out of her house. Sprinkling the books with a few drops of holy water from Ireland, Elizabeth put them in the light of the sun for a short while.

It seemed to do the trick because Elizabeth is perfectly comfortable with them now and is gleaning a better understanding of why her grandmothers were the way they were through reading them.

Take an intuitive tour through your home and office. Are there objects calling for cleansing because the energy needs transforming and transmuting? You can do it. Simply go to your wise heart and ask to be guided. Whatever works for you is correct. Keepsakes can be wonderful touchstones from which we gain great solace, pleasure, and strength, as long as their energy complements our own.

I have the wisdom and right to cleanse any object.

I trust my feelings and intuitions.

Savoring Our Souls

. . . .

BECAUSE THE DEMANDS OF DAY-TO-DAY LIFE
have a way of dulling our spirits and cutting us
off from our hearts, it's essential that we find
ways to reinstate solitude into our lives and,
through it, experience the beauty of heart and
soul. One day, while suffering from solitude
starvation, I ran across a poem in which the
poet talked about wandering alone through his
house savoring and kissing the fallen crumbs of
his soul.

I smiled as I read the poem because it valida-
ted the feelings I often have while home alone.
I wander—touching, appreciating, remembering, singing, gathering, and kissing the fallen
crumbs of my soul. Very often this is the time
that I choose to change the symbols in the
miniature Zen sand garden given to me by my
son. A simple task, taking only a few minutes at
the most, but nonetheless a richly replenishing
ritual in which I savor my soul.

If your soul has been dropping a trail of
crumbs as it accompanies your body through
its days, how would you like to savor and
nourish it? Can you arrange for some solitary

time at home in which you sweep up and kiss your soul crumbs?

Gently close your eyes and imagine a time in your own home when you are blessed by the renewal of solitude. Cherish it. Wander or sit quietly. Give yourself the gift of enjoying the solitude in ways that warm your heart, fill your spirit, and revitalize your soul.

It is a sacred assignment to rescue the crumbs of our souls that have been kicked under the table by too much activity and too little aloneness, and to collect and kiss them "all better."

I need and deserve time alone.

I am adept at balancing time alone and time with others.

Awakening
to
Wisdom

When sleeping women wake,
mountains move.

—Chinese proverb

WE ARE ALL AWARE THAT THERE ARE many mountains in need of moving. Mountains of ignorance and intolerance need to be transformed into peaks of understanding and acceptance, mountains of materialism must be lowered, and mountains of inequality must be transformed into partnership, respect, and egalitarianism.

We who bear the feminine qualities of compassion, intuition, and inclusion are called to awaken to our own prodigious wisdom and to move the mountains that block our paths and obliterate both Brother Sun and Sister Moon. Through our wisdom, we can fashion a powerfully creative and joyful life for ourselves and institute changes that will build a better world for our children and their children's children.

As with everything else, awakening to wisdom begins with ourselves as we realize that each of us is a creation of the Divine and therefore an expression and fulfillment of Divine purpose. As they say in Hawaii, "God don't make junk!" Far from being junk, at the center of our souls, we are innately, inherently, and incredibly wise. When we awaken to and act from our wisdom, mountains will move and the Divine will smile with satisfaction.

Becoming a Wisdom Gatherer

THE ANCIENT TERMINOLOGY FOR THE stages of a woman's life—Maiden, Mother, and Crone—needs to be expanded now that women are living much longer. Inserted between Mother and Crone is a necessary and fulfilling stage that I call Wisdom Gatherer.

Of course we gather wisdom all through our lives, but in keeping with the saying, "Given enough time and nourishment, sage will replace wild oats in the garden of life," midlife usually provides more opportunities for cultivating sage-filled wisdom than do the previous stages of Maiden or Mother. In the first, we are rightly cultivating ourselves; who we are, what we believe, and what values we hold dear. As Mothers, we often concentrate more on cultivating and nourishing the lives of others; if not children, then career, mate, or personal dreams.

The Wisdom Gatherer period is often the time when women wake and mountains begin to move. In this phase, our souls invite us to mature in spirit, acknowledge and build on our unique gifts and talents, and glean wisdom from our experiences through thoughtful contemplation. Ideally, as a Wisdom Gatherer, we take measure of ourselves—gently, realistically, and with honor—and in so doing, we see ourselves as highly capable and truly miraculous beings. During this period we cull all that we have learned and all that we intuitively know. Such introspection ushers us through the age of Wisdom Gatherer toward the eventual crown of Cronedom, or Eldership.

No matter what age you are, you can gather wisdom. Imagine yourself carrying a beautiful, handwoven basket as you move through the garden of life. Each circumstance, experience, and relationship has the potential for becoming a stunning blossom of compassion or a fragrant bundle of sage.

Think about the wisdom that you have gathered thus far. Give yourself credit for the ways in which you have grown and blossomed and for the ways that you've helped others grow. Appreciating ourselves each day gives us the courage to gather the seeds and stomp through the fertilizer, both of which are necessary to keep our garden of wisdom growing.

Each experience has within it a seed of wisdom.

I gather wisdom as I go through life.

Tending the Creative Fires

. . . .

OF ALL THE QUALITIES IN OUR BEING, THE one that is the most Godlike is creativity. Creativity is wisdom in action—a powerful, intangible, and deeply spiritual birthright.

We are born from the Creator to create, and, therefore, are fired by a primal desire to express our unique and individual creativity. Our universe is continually creating itself, and our bodies are in a constant state of re-creation. As an example: skin, scrapped, seared, or sliced immediately begins to create new skin. We take it for granted. Yet, such re-creation is an unconscious, instinctual miracle.

Consciously, our compulsion to create is no less compelling. Although our creative fires may have been dampened from our life circumstances up to this point, they are waiting, smoldering for us to rebuild them. Because creativity and wisdom are fraternal twins, tending our creative fires is a wonderful way to ignite and awaken to our wisdom. "Why should we all use our creative powers . . . ?" asks writer, Brenda Ueland, "Because there is nothing that makes people so generous, joyful, lively, bold and compassionate, so indifferent to fighting and the accumulation of objects and money." Sounds Godlike to me.

With quiet excitement, close your eyes and begin to deepen your breath. As you inhale say, "I am," and as you exhale say, "creative." I am . . . creative. I am . . . creative. Relaxing softly into the center of your being, visualize yourself tending a beautiful, vibrant, but in-control fire. Enjoy it in whatever ways feel good to you. This is your creative fire. What sparks need fanning? What new logs are yearning to be added? What passionate part of this fire needs to express itself more freely in order to feed your soul?

We are created in God's image. Would that not mean that one of our most natural gifts is to express creativity? Give yourself the gift of kindling the flames of your creativity, the light of which will illuminate your wisdom.

My creativity is wise, wonderful, and fun.

I make time to express my creativity.

Mining the Gold of Dreams

. . . .

DREAMS ARE A DIRECT PIPELINE FROM THE Divine. Although dreams are sometimes purely entertainment, very often they are symbolic wisdom lessons graphically showing us what is right and wrong in our lives and offering previews of coming attractions as well as hints about pitfalls that may dot our path. Reoccurring dreams are especially important wisdom teachers imploring us to pay attention.

Dreams may be the Spirit's easiest channel through which to communicate with us, but they are also the most elusive. Who hasn't awakened from a profoundly moving dream only to have its substance immediately quicksilver out of reach? If remembering dreams doesn't come naturally to us, we can train ourselves to become good at it.

Teaching ourselves to seize evasive dream messages is a two-layered process. On the spiritual/mind level, we need to set our intention and instruct our conscious mind to remember our dreams clearly. Before going to sleep, it's important to reaffirm the intention to remember and consciously welcome dreams as wisdom tools. We can then ask our higher selves or guardian angels for help.

On a physical level, it's usually a must to have paper and pen beside the bed to write down at least a memory jog, but *before moving even a fraction* immediately replay the dream. Movement shakes many dreams right out of awareness. Title your dreams and journal with and about them. Remember, you are your own best expert for interpreting your dreams.

Unless we are naturally adept at it, dream harvesting takes consistent practice and commitment. For many people, it's easy at times and almost impossible at others. Congratulate yourself for recalling even tiny fragments or remembering the barest hint of a feeling evoked by a dream. Becoming aware of our dreams creates the opportunity for nightly showers of Divine influence.

I effortlessly remember my dreams.

My dreams are a source of pleasure, affirmation, and instruction.

Living Our Dreams

. . . .

THE HEIGHT OF WISDOM IS BEING WILLING to live out our dreams, for they are urgings from our souls encouraging us to progress in the way that is right for us.

If we have lost track of our aspirations, those we had in childhood were often the wisdom of our souls telling us what our hearts desired. As children we were still close to the Source and, therefore, our dreams were very important sign posts. But a child intuitively knows whether her aspirations will be heard or denied by her family, and, if ours were denied, we may have learned to ignore them and live another person's dreams or let dreams go altogether.

Irene de Castillejo, in her book *Knowing Woman*, underscored the importance of living our own dreams: "Life insists on being lived, and anything that belongs to life which is allowed to lie dormant has to be lived by someone else. If we do not accept our shadow we force our children to carry the burden of our undeveloped capacities. They may become mediocre scientists or artists because we denied our own talents."

Right now, very gently, but with total honesty, ask yourself, "Am I trying to live out an unexpressed dream of a parent or other person in my life?" "Is a child of *mine* living out a talent that I have not developed?" and "Am I letting dreams lie dormant?"

If you suspect the answers may be yes or if you're unsure about what your own dreams are, close your eyes for a moment and allow your mind to roam back to the years when you were a kid. What did you long to be when you grew up? Who were your heroines? What books or television programs did you relate to? What dreams have you given up as impractical? Please listen to the soul-call of your dreams and creatively find ways to bring them to fruition.

I have the wisdom to bring my dreams and aspirations to fruition.

Each day my dreams become clearer to me.

Finding Work with Heart

. . . .

AT SOME DEEP LEVEL, EVERY ONE OF US wants to be of service to the world through meaningful work. But often finding that work is elusive, and we wander from job to job or stay in a dead-end job, never quite connecting to our soul's purpose.

The issue was front and center for me during my divorce. Because my self-esteem had to reach up to touch bottom at the time and I had only worked spasmodically during my marriage, I had no idea what I could do. However, in the midst of my terror, constantly and doggedly— without even a glimmer of faith on many occasions—I affirmed, "Each day I become clearer as to the work that is right for me in God's eyes." and prayed, "Help me have the clarity to see and hear the message, and the guts to follow through with it!"

There was never a bolt of lightening scorching "Thou shalt be a therapist," onto my brain, which was a good thing because I probably would have replied in horror, "I can't possibly be a therapist, but I sure do need one!" No, my prayers were answered one tiny little nudge at a time, baby-steps that I could garner the courage to take.

In order for you to get a sense of how to find meaningful soul-work, ask yourself the following questions: What do you find meaningful in life? What does your heart long to contribute to the world? What services are you equipped to provide? Who needs them? and, Do you want to give them? If you won a big lotto drawing, what would you do? Would that feel meaningful to you in the long run?

Although it is sometimes difficult, please trust that the wisdom within you *knows* what work is right for you. Today, ask God, your angels, and your soul-Self for help in arranging the perfect, right work for you.

Each day I become clearer as to the work that is right for me in God's eyes.

I open myself to finding and accepting work with heart.

Clearing Away the Cobwebs

. . . .

MY DAD USED TO SAY, "I'M GOING OUT TO
blow the stink off and clear away the cobwebs,"
when leaving the house for a walk or bike ride. I
don't know about the stink, but it's a well-
known fact that exercise helps our bodies work
more efficiently and clears the cobwebs from
our minds. A friend of mine who works with elderly people says it is amazing how just a little
bit of exercise helps her residents to sleep better, feel less depressed, and sharpen their mental
acumen. Rumor has it that some have also
rekindled their interest in romance.

It's especially wonderful when we can exercise outdoors where there is the opportunity to
immerse ourselves in beauty and greet other
people. Actually, we might get ourselves moving better if we changed the idea of "exercise"
to something with less drudgery attached to it
such as, "I'm going out to say 'hi' to Mother Nature," or "I'll be playing on the treadmill for the
next twenty minutes." No matter what form of
movement we choose, it needs to have an element of fun, adventure, or pleasure attached. It's
okay if the pleasure is as subtle as feeling a little

more alert. That's great. That's clearing away cobwebs.

If you already exercise and enjoy it, wonderful. If you don't, what can you do today to move your body just a little? Put on some music and dance a step or two? Walk down the stairs when going to lunch? Stretch the muscles in your neck and arms? Bodies, as well as minds and hearts, need to be stretched regularly.

In order to clear away the cobwebs, energize ourselves, and better access the wisdom of our intuition *and* our intellect, we need to give ourselves the gift of daily, enjoyable movement. Our bodies, hearts, and minds will all be thankful.

I exercise and enjoy it.
I love my body, heart, and mind,
and I exercise them daily.

Freeing Inner Elders

. . . .

EACH OF US HAS WITHIN HER EMISSARIES OF Light, inner elders who need to be recognized and claimed as we awaken to our wisdom. We have been so brainwashed by puritanical facets of our culture into believing that we are innately sinful and shameful beings that we tend to negate, ignore, and distrust our light-filled, divine selves. But don't be surprised if you meet a mystic, priestess, artist, philosopher, or gathering of wise elders as you explore the depths and heights of your inner self.

The Light is within us. We are asked to know ourselves, sunbeams and shadows alike, and, through love and acceptance, transform our shadow material, liberating its life force to become a source of light, vitality, and power. The diamond of our being sparkles more brilliantly when all facets are turned toward the light.

Our inner elders retain their innocence and divinity no matter what wounds we may have sustained in the school of life. As reflections of the Beloved's fire, Emissaries of Light are eternally willing to illuminate our paths. Opening to them and accepting their reality invites their wisdom to guide us. When set free, the elders of our souls can guide us in our quest for re-union with God.

Close your eyes and gently encourage your body to relax and your mind to quiet. Breathe deeply in through your nose and out through your mouth. Sink ever more deeply into the soft silence. As you feel ready, see or sense yourself in the midst of a gathering of wise elders. One or two of them may be clearer to you than the others. If you don't feel blessed by their presence, allow them to fade and invite in others with whom you feel absolutely loved. Immerse yourself in their love, honoring the fact that these elders are an integral part of your vast storehouse of wisdom.

I have within me a vast storehouse of wisdom.

*I and my Emissaries of Light
dance joyfully with the Beloved.*

Integrating the Black Madonna

. . . .

STATUES AND OTHER IMAGES OF THE BLACK
Madonna abound in the lowliest chapels and
most grandiose cathedrals in Europe. These
dark relics represent woman's essential, but
much maligned shadow aspects—the powerful,
earthy, humorous, lusty, fertile, disciplined, and
outspoken qualities that were stripped from the
Virgin Mary in the first few centuries A.D. Mary
was not always portrayed as a meek, long-suf-
fering, and submissive woman, however. To
many who trust their intuition, Mary was, and
is, viewed as the feminine aspect of God; a
powerful, compassionate, and wise deity.

The Black Madonna and the Virgin Mary
represent two halves of a whole Divine Feminine, a sacred partnership. Actually, in our
universe, everything is complemented by an
opposite. For instance, male and female must
combine to reproduce, and the synergy of dark
and light creates night and day. But a more al-
chemical symbol for the synergistic combina-
tion of opposites is the yin-yang sign. In it,
light and shadow fit together in a graceful
curve—each containing a circle of the other
within itself. Intertwined, they form a perfect

circle, which is the universal symbol of wholeness and infinity.

We, too, carry the same complementary opposites represented by the Black Madonna and the Virgin Mary. In order to form a balanced whole, we need to integrate both within our psyches and spirits. Do you acknowledge the powerful qualities of the Black Madonna within you? Do you allow the soft gentleness of the Virgin to express through you? Working on integrating the power of the Black Madonna is one of my lifelong tasks, and one that I didn't make much progress with until I was over fifty.

Individually and worldwide, we need both the earthy and the ethereal, the power and the compassion, and the dark and the light. We can integrate and act from both.

I accept all aspects of myself.
I constructively express both the light and dark within me.

Gleaning from Mistakes
and Failures

. . . .

AS AMERICAN POLITICAL ACTIVIST DOROTHY
McCall says, "One cannot have wisdom without living life." Because we are human and falli-
ble, throwing ourselves enthusiastically into the
business of living naturally means that we will
stumble and fall occasionally. Real people living
real lives make mistakes and experience failure.
It's what we do with our mistakes and failures
that makes the difference. If we get caught in
the perfectionist's lament of "If I can't do it perfectly, I won't do it at all," or if we berate ourselves to such an extent that we're too
frightened to try new things, we're not gleaning
the valuable lessons inherent in our setbacks.

If, on the other hand, we realize that perfection does not tolerate mistakes whereas excellence incorporates mistakes and learns from
them, we can toss perfectionism in the garbage
and glean value from failure. We're here to
learn. With just a small tilt in attitude, moving
from the need to appear perfect to the willingness to see mistakes as opportunities for great

growth and learning, we can make our lives so much more serene and fun.

Deciding to commit to excellence instead of perfection, we can welcome our mistakes with a lighter attitude and let them shed light on our progressive path toward wisdom. We can "lighten up!" as one of the most profound spiritual colloquialisms of our day encourages.

Write a list of any persistent shoulds and oughts that keep at least one of your feet solidly perched on the precarious platform of perfectionism. Write another, more life-friendly message, giving yourself permission to *acquire* skills and *learn* lessons through trial and error. Symbolically, or literally, toss your first list in the garbage.

On the sea of life, we're all in the same boat, and very few of us arrived automatically knowing how to row or set the sails.

I gently encourage myself to
learn from mistakes and failures.
I try to "lighten up" my heavy attitudes.

Emulating the Willow

. . . .

*That the yielding conquers the resistant and
the soft conquers the hard is a fact known to
all [wo]men, yet utilized by none.*

—Lao Tzu

SEATED BENEATH A LARGE WILLOW TREE
watching its leafy fingertips lightly brushing the
surface of a small pond, I had a compelling desire to become her student. Silently, I implored,
"Please teach me to be unaffected by life's
storms through wisely yielding to their turbu-
lence. Show me, dear sister, how to conquer the
hard attitudes of some people by softening my
own. Help me stop resisting philosophies and
opinions that I find righteous and intolerable
and, instead, shine light and impersonal love
upon their bearers. Help me dance with the
winds of Spirit and not stiffen in my own beliefs
of how things should be evolving."

How can we be a willow but not a wimp? So
often resistance appears to be the only way, and
conquering through soft yielding seems merely
a fantasy. We can learn the wisdom of the willow and open our hearts to its counsel. For a

few moments give yourself the joy of imagining that you are a beautiful, strong, and flexible willow tree.

Visualize an exquisite setting for yourself as the most feminine of trees. Feel your roots firmly implanted on the breast of Mother Earth, and, if you'd like, get up and allow your body to sway as if the wind were playing (or raging) through your graceful branches. Soak in the sense of willowness. Flexibility, strength, beauty, resilience, durability, grace, acceptance, wisdom—all of these qualities are hers. All are also yours. Where in your life do you need to emulate the willow more than you currently are? From the depths of your wise feminine heart, can you encourage yourself to become more willowlike in attitude and action?

I am both flexible and strong.
I easily dance with the winds of life.

Being in the Flow

. . . .

ARTISTS OF ALL KINDS—WRITERS, PAINTERS, counselors, musician, parents, lovers, sculptors, teachers, entrepreneurs—often speak of their very creative times as "being in the flow." While in the flow, life functions like a beautifully choreographed ice skating routine. Effortlessly, we glide through a project or conversation as if lubricated by angel oil. It feels great!

While some of those times are gifts of grace, more often we have primed the pump by having positive attitudes as well as following through with our commitment to sit at the computer, teach the class, do one more parental chore, or quiet our mind through solitude, meditation, and introspection. Mentally and physically, we've prepared ourselves and made a commitment. As a result, the magical "flow" answers our call.

Becoming increasingly gentle with who we really are will help us remain in the flow of our lives rather than continually thrashing exhaustedly against the current. We grow into the wisdom of going with the flow by accepting and trusting our own excellence and the benevolence of the Divine.

Patty, a wise friend of mine, once told me that her most profound workshop experience came from a group singing "Row, row, row your boat gently down the stream" for over a half hour. At first, she groused to herself what a colossal waste of time and money this was, but she finally began to flow along *with* the current of the experience and *got*, at a deep gut level, how much—and not at all merrily—she tried to swim against the current in her daily life. For Patty, that little ditty became a mantra that helped her learn to live in the flow of life.

Having the wisdom to tap into the artistry of life by rowing our boats gently *down* the stream brings increasing freedom to our spirits and solace to our souls.

I row gently and merrily downstream.

*I have the wisdom and courage to trust both
God and myself.*

Planting Where We
Are Blooming

. . . .

WE'VE ALL HEARD THE WONDERFUL LITTLE aphorism, "Bloom where you are planted." However, the opposite is equally true. We have already planted seeds of insight, compassion, and inspiration where we are blooming. In precisely the areas where we naturally excel or have diligently worked to be able to shine, others are benefiting from the fruits and flowers of our accrued wisdom.

For example, Bobbie, who is a wonderful parent, has written an equally wonderful parenting book; Bonnie, who has absolutely fallen in love with grandparenting, gives classes to grandparents on the art of mentoring grandchildren; and, Carolyn, who has always loved being around elderly people, is now shepherding her mother toward heaven's gate. Each of these women is planting a garden for others where they, themselves, already bloom. In Carolyn's case, not only is she planting seeds for a grace-filled death for her mom, but she is sowing the seeds of her own future in which she hopes to work in the field of gerontology.

Where are you already blooming? In what field do you flower exceptionally well? Where does your wisdom shine brightly?

Take a few moments now to meditate on ways and places in which you are in full bloom. If you find it difficult to be aware of your own flowering, imagine that your dearest friend is telling you how she perceives your blooming. What seeds of wisdom are you now planting, and what others can you plant in order to beautify the garden of life?

Be generously honest, for one of the most significant things women can do is awaken to, welcome, and accept their own wisdom. Only then can we plant seeds of service and share our fertile wisdom and compassion for the benefit of those whom we love and those whom we may never meet.

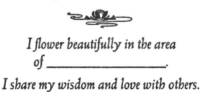

I flower beautifully in the area
of _____.

I share my wisdom and love with others.

Enrolling
in
Saint's School

*One thing that comes out of myths is
that at the bottom of the abyss comes the
voice of salvation. The black moment is
the moment when the real message of
transformation is going to come. At the
darkest moment comes the light.*

—Joseph Campbell

I ONCE HEARD STEPHEN LEVINE TELL A newly diagnosed ALS patient that, through his illness, he had been enrolled in Saint's School. We all have the option of enrolling in Saint's School when called upon to grapple with trauma, pain, and death. It's an excellent choice to view crises and afflictions as a school in which we can hone our souls, for how we handle the lessons life presents determines whether we eventually attain the serenity and peace of mind of a saint or endure the demons of agitation, bitterness, resentment, and depression.

Crisis is a part of the human cycle. We ascend, flourish, bear fruit, and then, seemingly as an answer to the law of gravity, we arch, hit a plateau, descend, and die to the part of us wounded in crisis. Because feminine energy is deeply aware of and in tune with cycles, crisis is best handled by the Sacred Feminine within us. She, in her wisdom, knows that crisis is followed by rebirth. When a part of us—an old pattern, an expectation, a role, a loved one—is washed away in the alchemy of crisis, new parts of our being and new possibilities for our lives are conceived and born. Trauma and transformation walk hand in hand. In joy, we are blessed, and, through sorrow we are given the opportunity to become a blessing.

Kissing the Darkness

. . . .

AS HUMAN BEINGS, WE ARE ALL ENROLLED IN
Saint's School at some time or other. There are
daily lessons to learn and daily losses to release,
but many of us seem to study these assignments
most often under the blanket of night.

Night blurs the revealing corners of day, ob-
scuring the familiar pegs upon which we hang
our facades. Stoic masks dissolve as our most
fundamental fears parade in the darkness.
Stripped of day's bright distractions, night finds
us alone, its black mirror reflecting and magni-
fying our deepest concerns. In the profound
shadows of night, the apocalypse horses of iso-
lation and despair may try to drag us from our
daytime strength into a pit of relentless anxiety
and self-pity.

However, we can choose, instead, to descend to the heights of our soul by kissing the
darkness hello. We can embrace the fertility of
"night school" by blessing our pain while exploring the insights that it offers. Kissing the
darkness invites it to reveal its mysteries to us,
but kicking the darkness away creates unre-
solved issues which fester into chronic pain and

limitations. For, as we all know but must relearn over and over, resistance only magnifies pain.

If you are currently taking night classes in Saint's School, gently prepare by making a plan to comfort yourself when sleep will not come and darkness is your only company. Perhaps a cup of your favorite tea ready to be brewed, candles waiting to be lighted, a journal and pen at the ready, and a cozy afghan will help give you the courage to glean the wisdom offered by your present experience.

When, through crisis, loss, or chaos, we rotate away from the light of our being, much like the earth rotates away from the sun at night, it's best to kiss the darkness as we fall under its shadow and open to our pain and meet it in the depths of our wise hearts. Doing so ensures the dawn of a new day.

I have the courage to explore the lessons revealed in the fertile darkness.

I accept both light and dark in my life.

Being Responsible to *Our Crises, Not* for *Them*

. . . .

ACCEPTANCE OF SUFFERING CHANGES CRISIS from tormentor to teacher. True acceptance, with an eye and ear toward what we can learn from a crisis, has nothing to do with being a helpless victim of circumstances. Rarely, if ever, is there anything to gain from viewing ourselves as a victim, but there is everything to gain from seeing ourselves as a student in each situation.

Some popular philosophies believe that we create everything that happens to us, and to a certain extent that's probably true, but surely Life and Spirit are so mysterious and unfathomable that it's a little grandiose of us to believe that we know exactly what creates what.

In reality, we can't always choose what will happen to us, or even *in* us, but we are free to choose how we will respond. We *can* choose to learn from everything that happens to us. As students in the school of life, we are responsible *to* our crises. What can we learn from them? How can we grow through them?

It's important that we look at illness or other crises as an educator giving us the opportunity to enrich our spirits and expand our consciousness and not to judgmentally label them as something we've created out of an inevitable flaw within ourselves. Yes, we do things and feel feelings that deplete our immune systems and create a climate in which illness can flourish, and it's very important that we pay attention to taking care of our bodies and our beliefs. But, if we badger ourselves mercilessly about being responsible for crises, we often end up paralyzed by guilt and, consequently, learn nothing.

There is also the possibility that our crises are lessons we signed up for on a spiritual level; opportunities to advance our soul by choosing gentleness, empowerment, and serenity over judgment, victimization, or bitchiness. Who knows? None of us, really. What we do know is that we're all enrolled in Saint's School and we learn best when treated with gentle kindness.

I forgive myself for having crises.
Although I may not like them, I do learn from crises.

Anointing Ourselves with Tears

AS THE TURKISH PROVERB STATES, "SHE THAT conceals her grief finds no remedy for it." Grief concealed becomes grief congealed. Sorrow and pain shift and heal more readily when we anoint ourselves with the balm of tears.

It's a well-known scientific fact that tears shed in grief, anger, hopelessness, and contrition contain significant toxins, whereas tears shed in joy and awe do not. From these findings, it appears that tears have the capacity to cleanse the body. I believe they can cleanse the soul as well. On occasion we've all probably known that we needed a "good" cry. We feel the buildup of energy and intuitively know that release can be found in the goodness of tears. If we allow ourselves to weep, we often feel refreshed and revitalized.

Thirteenth-century German mystic, Mechthild of Magdeburg, wrote that "tears are a passing on of the river of grace." She believed that tears were God's divine energy flowing through us. Wouldn't it be wonderful if we could move into the heart of our feelings and let warm, moist tears cleanse our bodies and anoint our souls?

"Jesus wept" is the shortest verse in the Bible, set off to underscore its significance, I presume. Who was more in the river of grace than the enlightened Christ? His example is a good one for us to follow.

When you have a few undisturbed minutes, gently put your hands over your heart and breathe in the words "I love you" and "I long for your healing." As you breathe deeply, give yourself permission to let tears flow freely if they want to come. It isn't necessary to know what your tears are about; it's simply important to release them.

There's a little story that suggests God saves each of our tears, turns them into pearls, and presents them to us when we enter heaven. Anointing ourselves with tears not only aids in healing, but allows us to add to our celestial string of pearls.

I gently allow myself to cry needed tears.

The Beloved cherishes my tears.

Touching the Hem

. . . .

IT'S VERY IMPORTANT, AS WE MOVE THROUGH the morass of confusion and consternation often prevalent in Saint's School, that we have taproots from which to draw energy, support, and solace.

Although we need other people whom we can count on to support us, God, angels, and other ethereal beings are happy to provide these comforts when we open ourselves to them and ask for their help. In the Bible, followers of Christ believed that if they touched the hem of his robe, they would be healed, and they were right. Part of our task in becoming women of spirit is to create a goodly supply of *internal* hems to touch, hands to hold, and arms to enfold us as we move toward greater wholeness.

If you're not comfortable using Christ as the symbol for an all-compassionate Being in the following meditation, please replace him with a Being of your own choosing. Allow your eyes to drift gently closed and visualize the thoughts of your mind and the feelings of your heart as white goose down feathers flung free from a ruptured pillow. Allow the feathers to settle quietly on the calm surface of a beautiful lotus pond. If any ornery feathers insist on staying airborne, go after them with amusement and tenderly coax them to land on the unruffled water. Invite Christ to be with you by the pond. In ways that feel nurturing to you, rest, rejuvenate, and heal in his presence.

In a particularly difficult time in my life, I gained great solace from picturing myself sitting on the ground beside Jeshua (Jesus' Aramaic name, and one that is less loaded for me) and leaning my head on his knee as he stroked my hair, while I fingered the hem of his garment.

A visualization of this type can help create an ongoing relationship with a loving Being that can become a taproot of strength and comfort for us.

I rest in the presence of a loving being.

I am loved and comforted,
and I freely love and comfort others.

Lifting the Rocks

. . . .

EVEN THOUGH WE CAN'T READILY SEE IT, life teems under rocks. Turn over a rock and notice all the little critters scurrying about, doing the business of living.

So it is with us—life is teeming beneath the rocks of our day-to-day existence. Whether we are suffering from the weight of accumulated fatigue or have been ripped from the very ground of our being, it's encouraging to remember that these are fertile times for spiritual growth. New life abounds as we gather the strength and energy to lift painful rocks and examine the underbelly of our own psyches and spirits. Such exploration definitely isn't easy, but it is necessary for the evolution of our souls. We need the dark, fertile, moist soil of crisis to define ourselves. Without struggle, there is no energy to break the shell encasing the seeds of our new self, the soul-self that we are becoming.

Vulnerability is wrapped around the axis of all pain. Therefore, as we go into the darkness, it's crucial to do so gently. Kicking over inner rocks with a vengeance and squashing the little bug beings revealed only causes our spirits to wisely move out of reach.

With gentleness in mind, close your eyes and imagine yourself as light as a feather on the breath of God. Supported by the Divine, effortlessly float to a beautiful place in nature. When you see a spot where you would like to glide to a stop, softly settle into the beauty. Beside you is a rock that represents an experience or belief that causes you pain. Holding fast to the awareness of the sacred opportunity for soul growth in all experiences, turn over your rock and gently examine the insights to be exposed in the fertile darkness.

Carl Jung reminds us, "There is no coming to consciousness without pain." Would that that were not true, but it usually is. What radiant spiritual possibilities lie in the shadows of your rocky pain waiting to be unearthed?

I am gentle with myself as I turn over the rocks of my psyche.

I open my heart to the opportunities inherent in pain and crisis.

Moving Toward Acceptance

. . . .

I LOVE THE NORSE SAYING, "CLOUDS MOVE." It reminds me that no matter how many clouds cover the sun, they will eventually leave. It is their nature, just as it is the nature of the human spirit to move out from under clouds and heal in the wake of crisis and trauma. Continually and consciously moving toward acceptance of people and circumstances over which we have no control creates an atmosphere that supports healing and transformation. Although acceptance isn't easy, it is facilitated when we re-form and re-frame crisis through re-wording how we think and talk about it.

A few simple, but helpful suggestions are:

1. Change "my" and "our" pain to "the" pain. *The* pain is less personal and more manageable.

2. Replace both the words and attitude of "Isn't it awful!" Instead, learn to say and believe, "That's good." We don't have to believe that something is good right away, and if we just can't bring ourselves to say "That's good," we can pray, "I can't yet see any good in this. Please help my vision clear and my trust return."

3. We can dis-identify with our feelings by remembering that at the core of ourselves is an

indestructible divinity—our soul-self—who understands and remains apart from the crucible of crisis (or, at least, remains unscathed and unscarred). We can help ourselves dis-identify with our pain and remember our Self by saying, "I have this feeling, but I am not this feeling. I am_____." I then fill that space with whatever feels the most healing. I use a "pure child of God" or "a strong and wise spiritual being." It varies with my need.

4. Remember, "This, too, shall pass." When this challenge has passed, what growth and insights will you have gleaned?

Clouds move, crises pass, wounds heal; acceptance helps.

*Difficult feelings flow through me
like clouds moving through the sky.*

I am a survivor and thriver.

Sanctifying Pain

. . . .

Though the soul's wounds heal, the scars remain.
God sees them not as blemishes but as honors.

—Julian of Norwich

MYSTICS AND PHILOSOPHERS AGREE THAT it is pain that seasons and strengthens our souls. Pain used as an impetus for soul growth and understanding is sanctified as a result. Staying open to the honors to be gained from pain is difficult at the onset of a wound. Our task, when first thrown to the mat, is to gently allow ourselves to grieve and, later when and if we're able, to be willing to open to the soul growth inherent in the experience.

When initially faced with the knowledge that my first marriage was on the rocks, I was devastated and obsessed with the searing pain that I felt. At first, if anyone had told me to open to the soul growth in this experience, I would have wanted to punch them out. Over time, and with much help, I was able to accept that, from this crisis, a new and better Sue might emerge. And that was the turning point.

For me, Jung's statement, "It is through the

wounds that light can come in" was absolutely true. In the fire of my pain was born the therapist I became, the spiritual seeker that I still am, and the person I quest to be. I can truthfully say that I feel extraordinarily blessed by the gifts that emanated from my divorce.

Paradoxically, there are still—and always will be—fragments of sadness to hold side by side with the gratitude. Sanctification of our pain requires that we embrace the paradox and give thanks for both the growth and sadness hidden in the mystery of Saint's School. Embracing all aspects of crisis makes it easier for our scars to become badges of honor.

Intermittently, life cracks us all open, and we heal stronger in the broken places. Today, what cracks and wounds would you like to invite the light to shine through by sanctifying the pain with growth and gratitude?

I accept joy and sorrow, alike, and learn from each.

I invite light to shine through my wounds,
blessing others.

Soothing the Soul with Ritual

RITUAL IS IMPORTANT DURING CRISIS FOR IT is the language of the soul. In difficult times, ritual can help us reaffirm our relationship with the Divine, satiate our thirst for spiritual sustenance, and augment our flagging trust in the goodness of life.

I was very inspired by the rituals Julianna, a young woman whom I met at an Elisabeth Kubler-Ross workshop, shared with me. Afflicted with Multiple Sclerosis (MS), Julianna used Goodbye Rituals to formalize the letting go of the activities and functions of her body that she lost as her disease progressed. The first was a ceremony celebrating the years that she had been an avid rock climber and guided disadvantaged kids on adventures such as Outward Bound. To help her both grieve and celebrate her curtailed outdoor activities, she invited some of the people with whom she had gone on those excursions to her home. They shared memories, stories, anger, frustration, and tears.

The final segment of Julianna's ceremony included dividing her gear among the young people present and symbolically burning maps of her favorite trails and rock climbing spots.

Julianna prayed that her feelings, fueled by the MS, be transformed and transmuted into acceptance and strength just as the maps were being transformed, by fire, into a different, more ethereal energy. Each time Julianna lost another activity or ability, she—with the help of her caretaker—ritualized the process of letting go and asked for God's help in living graciously until death. Not long before her death, she wrote me that creating and performing the rituals had been a major contributor to her eventual peace of mind and serenity. She graduated from Saint's School, Phi Beta Kappa, I bet.

Are there ways in which your soul could be soothed through ritual? If so, give yourself the blessing of creating one. It doesn't matter what we *do* in a ritual; our souls—the wise, inner source of our being—respond to our heartfelt intention.

I soothe my soul through ritual.
I am serene and have peace of mind.

Nurturing the Three F's

. . . .

As we move ever higher in our commitment to nurturing and enriching the spirit within us, we learn to make daily choices for love and to prioritize our lives accordingly.

In reevaluating what has value and meaning to them, almost all of the cancer and AIDS patients that Dr. Joan Borysenko has worked with come up with what she calls the Three F's: Faith, Family, and Friends. I would include oneself in the "Friends" category.

Each of these F's has to do with love—how we connect with and relate to the Divine, ourselves, and others. In my own hospice work, I've talked with many terminally ill people who've told me that, although their illness was killing them, it was also providing them with the incentive to live from their hearts as their top priority. Faced with imminent death, most of us don't decide to work more—unless our work is a source of creativity and meaning. What we usually realize, when setting final priorities, is that we want to make profoundly loving connections.

Long before death taps on our door, we can choose to orient our lives according to the

Three F's. Today, take a sheet of paper and at the top, jot down Family, Friends/Self, and Faith—or any other heading that comes to you. Thoughtfully and tenderly list under each column ways that you might choose to act differently if you, or any of the people in your life, were to be given only a year to live. I know this idea is commonplace, but actually performing the exercise can be extremely enlightening. Use it as a springboard for change, if needed, or as an affirmation, if appropriate.

Daily conscious decisions to choose love and drink from the restorative well of Faith, Family, and Friends helps assuage our spiritual thirst for fulfillment and meaningful connections with ourselves, others, and our Source.

I fill myself at the well of love.

I tenderly nurture my faith, family, and friends.

Polishing Golden Souls

OUR SOULS ARE GOLDEN, AND OUR BACK-grounds either encourage them to shine or help them to tarnish. For those of us who feel we have spots of tarnish on our souls, there are many ways to polish them back to their natural radiance.

No matter how desperately we may hope for a better yesterday, the reality of the past cannot be changed. But the wonderful news is that the energy of the past *can* be transformed and transmuted, changed and lifted into the light of God. Through the incredible wisdom and creativity of our imagination, we can pluck painful or limiting fragments of energy from the barbed wire fences of our past and release them to express their perfect, right energetic vibration.

I learned the following soul-buffing technique from my spiritual mother, Annabelle Woodard. This meditation can be used to change the energy of any painful past experience, but I'm going to use it here in what Annabelle calls, "Grafting a New Childhood." Please feel free to tailor the meditation to your own unique needs if you have no parental issues or if some other wound calls to you more clearly.

Make yourself comfortable and close your eyes. Focus your attention on your breath and allow it to deepen naturally. On the in-breath say, "I," and as you breathe out, say, "Invite healing." When you feel more relaxed and open, invite your mind to roam back into your childhood until you see or sense a scene that you would like to transform. Call in your guardian angels to protect and comfort you as you relive the scene as you remember it. And now ask the compassionate wisdom of your heart to help you craft a different scenario. The first step is to request that your ideal parents appear. With these new parents in place, redo the experience. You may change anything you want in order to create it exactly as you wish it had been, and, energetically speaking, you will make it so.

Transforming the energy of the past by recreating that which needs healing, burnishes our souls to a golden hue.

My soul is a golden reflection of Spirit.

I deserve love, and I am capable of transforming painful energy into loving energy.

Changing Form, Not Essence

WHILE WATCHING THE SUN SET OVER THE Pacific Ocean on the anniversary of my dad's death, I had a comforting thought. Similar to foam on the breast of the ocean, we individuals are like foam in the sea of creation: mysteries, uniquely defined for a short space of time, and then absorbed back into the Source.

When we grasp the reality that, no matter what form of foam we are, each of us is an integral part of the vast ocean and will become one with it in the natural ebb and flow of nature, fear loses its grip on us and our hearts open toward all of our brothers and sisters. Each form is equally ocean in essence—all important, precious, and sacred. There is no separation between us and God or between us and those we love who have changed from human form, even though visually and tactually there appears to be a separation.

There is a wonderful little chant that, when sung repeatedly, helps us hold onto the belief of oneness with the Divine. As with most chants, this one is very simple: "I am a bubble, make me the sea. Make me the sea, oh make me the sea. I am a bubble, make me the sea."

I was singing this song and thinking about my dad when I was filled with the absolute assurance that Essence is forever, and we are all essence. Words are often inadequate to describe a heartfelt insight, and I feel that frustration now as the memory surges through me but the feelings refuse to be translated onto the page. My bet is that you understand anyway.

Our souls, like little kids, love repetition and bloom brilliantly when sacred words and thoughts are repeated. Let yourself get celestially creative and make up a tune to "I am a bubble, make me the sea," or compose your own unique refrain and sing it silently or aloud as you go through your day today. It's especially beneficial when negative thoughts are wreaking havoc in your heart. Your chant may become your heart-song.

I am one with the Divine.

There is only the appearance of separation, not separation itself.

Walking Through *the Valley of the Shadow*

. . . .

WALKING THROUGH THE VALLEY OF THE shadow of death with someone can be a blessed experience, one that fills us with awe and gives us an undying belief in the eternal evolution of our souls. If sudden however, the death of a loved one will, for a time, cast us into the fires of acute emotional trauma.

However, both peaceful and shocking deaths can bring forth an emergence of heart and soul. Our hearts, broken open by grief, bear fruits of the Spirit in the same way a seed, broken open by nature, bears fruits that sustains the body. As M. C. Richards says, "If you live into the experience of grief or loss deeply, you will perceive that what has taken place is not discontinuity but metamorphosis."

An essential quest for us is to discover beliefs about death that nourish us, for our attitudes surrounding the inevitability of the body's extinction either help or hinder our spiritual growth. The deeper our faith in the evolution of our souls and the benevolence of the Divine, the greater our acceptance of all circumstances and the possibility of transformation in them.

In all of my work with death and dying, one thing stands out as the most important in walking *through* the valley rather than being *stuck* in the shadows. And that is overcoming the fear of death. Those who do have faith in the eternality of the soul are transformed through the process of both grieving and dying themselves. Conversely, those who believe death is the end, struggle to regain their equilibrium when facing death or bereavement, and sometimes never do.

When I was younger, death was not something I thought about; indeed, it was something I avoided out of fear. As I've aged, I can truthfully say that I have come to feel as Pearl S. Buck does, "You are only afraid because you don't know anything about death. . . . But someday you will wonder why you were afraid, even as today you wonder why you feared to be born." Like the caterpillar, we are called upon to overcome our fear of death and emerge from the darkness transformed into more beautiful spiritual beings.

I accept death as merely another form of life.

My soul is eternal and indestructible.

Dancing with the Dead

. . . .

IN SOME NATIVE AMERICAN TRADITIONS, IT IS believed that we dance with our ancestors along the Milky Way after we leave this life. So many of the stories I've heard and experiences I've had convince me that we don't have to leave this life in order to dance with those who have already departed. Although I've had several encounters with my mother's spirit since her death, I want to tell you about one particular "dance" that we shared.

Minutes after Mother's death, I was engulfed by a sense of euphoria that stayed with me constantly for ten days. Never before or since have I experienced such prolonged joy. At the time, I thought the feeling came from my relief at Mother's release from pain. Several years later, during a meditation, I casually asked why I had felt the way I had. Although I really didn't expect an answer, immediately an internal message came—clear as a bell: "It wasn't just relief, as you think, Honey. You brought me such comfort *during* the illness that I wanted to share with you a little of what I was feeling *after* it." If what I felt was death, it is truly a dance of ecstasy.

Befriending death allows our spirits much freer reign in life. Toward that end, please close your eyes and, in whatever way feels right to you, sink into a state of deep relaxation. In your mind's eye, transport yourself to a beautiful wooded glen beside a small crystal-clear pool. Gaze into the water and see, mirrored there, a reflection of your spiritual face. For a few moments, give yourself permission to leave the confines of your physical body, merge with the face in the pool, and rise to dance along the Milky Way. Feel the freedom. Enjoy. Be in joy. Give thanks. Celebrate.

Though our bodies die, our souls dance forever.

I am an eternal, spiritual being.

I am never alone.

Ascending
to
Gratitude

Gratitude is heaven itself.

—*William Blake*

GRATITUDE IS THE FINEST PRAYER OUR souls can utter. Gratitude is also an attitude. As with any attitude, it can be nurtured, cultivated, and changed if need be. Gratitude, like laughter and humor, lifts our spirits and hearts and encourages us to ascend into realms of joy and appreciation. It makes us thankful for the incredible gift of life that we've been given and for the people who have chosen to share it with us.

Gratitude gentles even the roughest roads and gives wings to the heart. Buoyed by gratitude, we can sail over most situations while keeping a healthy, and even joyful, perspective on the landscape of our lives. Gratitude is communion with God and graces our relationships with a high and holy soul-connection. Gratitude is meditation in action. Gratitude is the single most powerful medicine for physical, mental, and spiritual health for us individually, and for our planet as a whole.

Drinking the Sweet Nectar
of Gratitude

. . . .

WE ARE OFFSPRING OF THE ALMIGHTY,
filled with divine energy and powerful potential. As we gently learn to believe in our own
worth, gratitude for our unique individuality is
the result.

Wine can give us a high and, regrettably,
also a headache. Drinking deeply of gratitude,
on the other hand, is naturally intoxicating,
with no bad aftereffects. This sweet nectar of
the gods nurtures our ability to ascend into the
company of angels and live life from our hearts,
with freer access to our soul-energy.

It might help to realize the value of gratitude
toward ourselves if we were to visualize our
heart as a delicate treasure, hand-blown from
the rarest ethereal glass. A treasure valuable beyond imagining—fragile, irreplaceable, priceless, and ancient. There is *no* other like
it—infinitely precious, existing before time and
after infinity.

In reality, we *were* entrusted with such an in-
explicable treasure when we were given the gift
of life. We, and our wonderful hearts, are infi-

nitely strong, vastly vulnerable, deserving and needing the gentle touch of gratitude and love.

With your eyes closed, very gently put your hands over your heart and allow your breath to tenderly flow in and out of it. When you feel ready, ask to be given a symbol for your heart. Hold the symbol that you see or sense as carefully and gently as you would a priceless Fabergé egg. Beholding the wonder of your symbol, allow gratitude to flow through you, permeating the very cells of your being. Make a commitment with yourself to cherish and appreciate your heart-self.

We also need to be especially gentle with ourselves when we misplace our sense of gratitude. We are human, and, when the pain in our hearts becomes acute, we sometimes forget to be grateful. That's okay, because we can always reclaim our gratitude. And as we remember to drink the sweet nectar of gratitude toward ourselves, the cup naturally passes to those whom we love.

I am infinitely grateful for my heart and soul.
Daily, I drink the sweet nectar of gratitude.

Nibbling Back to God's Pastures

. . . .

DISTRACTED AND OVERBUSY, WE CAN EASILY become like sheep and, with our heads down, inadvertently nibble our way out of God's pastures. Often, when we take the time to look up, we're astounded at how far afield we've wandered. Fortunately, gratitude is a surefire way to nibble our way back when we meander away from our spiritual home.

In the wake of losing her job, Ruth, a single woman in her thirties, battled insomnia during the night and exhaustion spiked with panic during the day. Finally, in desperation, she got up one late evening and numbly made a list of all the things that she had to be thankful for. Although she didn't *feel* thankful, she prayed for the strength to overcome her fear and the grace to experience gratitude. No bolts of lightening struck that night, but when she returned to bed, she did fall asleep. Getting up and at least thinking about being thankful became a ritual for Ruth when sleep eluded her. Slowly—nibble by minuscule nibble—she began to really feel gratitude and, with it, the ballast of hope.

It's said that "Thank-you" is the most powerful prayer, and thank-yous are invariably connected with gratitude. The following exercise can help illuminate the path back to the pastures for which we yearn.

Very quickly jot down all of the things for which you are thankful. The list may include people, ideas, objects—whatever pops into your mind. Once you have your list, say a tiny thank you for each item on the paper.

To be really creative, make a Thank-You Box and toss in ideas or experiences for which you are thankful every day. In the finest sense of the word, this is a Prayer Box; each slip of paper placed in it and every little "thank-you" murmured over it are nibbles back toward God's pastures.

God waits for us by the gates of gratitude.

I am grateful for all that I am and all that I have been.

I am at home in God.

Cultivating Optimism

· ·

AN OPTIMISTIC ATTITUDE INVITES AN INFLUX of positive energy into ourselves. You might say that optimism is the yeast in the bread of life. With it we rise, without it our spirits fall flat.

By her own admission, Cecilia is a recovering pessimist. She came by it naturally through the litanies she often heard repeated by her family of origin: "Isn't that terrible? Wouldn't you know it" (usually accompanied by a sigh); "Well, what can you expect from a politician, teenager, mailman . . ." (or whatever hapless person was skewered at the moment); "It doesn't get much worse than this," and, finally, "Lord knows I tried!" (always accompanied by a sigh).

After living in another state for several years, Cecilia was having lunch in her hometown with her aunt, cousin, and mother. Because she had been away, she was struck by the pessimistic and negative tenor of the talk around the table as never before. "I sat there stunned," she told me, "nauseated, heavyhearted, and longing to escape. Starting right then, I vowed to become an optimist." It must have worked because Cecilia is fun to be around, and two of the adjectives often used to describe her are "optimistic" and "lighthearted."

Darkness and heaviness weigh us down and clog our hearts and arteries physically, emotionally, and spiritually. An Irish proverb states, "A light heart lives long," but afflicted by a dark attitude and a heavy heart, life, no matter how long it really is, *seems* endless, dreary, and bleak.

Luckily, neither heavyheartedness nor a pessimistic attitude needs to be a life-sentence. We can learn to "enlighten up" as an astute bumper sticker teaches. We can transform a bad habit into a good one by consistently and gently monitoring our self-talk and changing any negative pessimism we spot to positive optimism. We can revive our spirits by cultivating optimism.

I am lighthearted and optimistic.

Life is great.

Distilling Wine
from Sour Grapes

IN AESOP'S FABLE, *THE FOX*, AFTER FUTILE efforts to reach a juicy clump of grapes, scorns them as being sour. I can imagine him haughtily turning up his nose and swishing his tail as he harrumphs away, belittling the coveted fruit only because he can't have it.

How often do we, like Mr. Fox, sully our spirits by falling prey to the sour-grape syndrome of jealousy, envy, or judgment of ourselves as not being up to snuff? I for one was plagued by jealousy as a youngster, and it made my life—and me, I suspect—miserable. Luckily, sour grapes are no longer a daily snack.

Another success story that I'd like to share with you concerns fraternal twins, Penny and Pam. The girls couldn't have been more disparate if they'd been born in different families. For most of their childhood, Pam was terribly jealous of Penny and, because of her feelings of inferiority, belittled her sister both in private and in public, generally trying to make her life miserable. At her wits end, Penny came to see me when she was a junior in high school. In therapy, she learned how to protect herself from her sister's barbs while also accepting responsibility for her part of the sour-grape syndrome.

Eventually, Pam joined her sister in therapy. A great deal of their work concentrated on increasing their individual self-esteem, being thankful for their differences, and viewing dissimilarities as ways to complement each other rather than compete. As adults, Pam and Penny continue to be completely different from each other, but they also enjoy a full-bodied and robust friendship.

If you find a sour grape fermenting in your mouth, it's wise to immediately change its essence with a little prayer or thought of gratitude. Wine distilled from sour grapes is often sweeter because of the spiritual discipline of thankfulness required to make the transformation.

I am happy being exactly who I am.

I am thankful for all that comes my way and look for the good in it.

Kissing the Joy

. . . .

TO POUR THE SACRED WATER OF THE Beloved upon our spirits we must first, *recognize* joy as it brushes lightly against our souls, and second, *appreciate* joy in the moment without trying to snatch it and bury it in the backyard like a bone. William Blake describes this beautifully in his poem, "Kiss the Joy as It Flies."

> *He who binds to himself a joy*
> *Does the winged life destroy;*
> *But he who kisses the joy as it flies*
> *Lives in eternity's sunrise.*

If we feel less joy in our lives than we do guilt, obligation, resentment, exhaustion, or depression, it probably means that a spiritual tune-up is in order. We may simply need to recalibrate our ability to tune into joy as it flits unobtrusively by the windows of our souls.

Daily, joy sits patiently on the sill, gently fanning its wings waiting for us to recognize it. But, oblivious or blinded by our own agenda, we sometimes act as C. S. Lewis lamented to a friend, "It seems to me that we often, almost sulkily, reject the good that God offers us because, at that moment, we expected some other good."

After tuning our intention toward recognizing the good that God offers, it's important that we hold its fragile essence in an open hand, accepting and appreciating it now, not crushing it in a clenched fist in hopes of preserving it for later.

That true joy is sufficient unto the moment is hard to remember. I know, because Blake's poem settled itself in my broken heart during a black period when joy was hard to come by. Nonetheless, his poem became a spiritual challenge to me. For its inspiration, I am eternally grateful. Appreciating and then releasing joy allows us, paradoxically, to truly savor it.

I open my eyes to joy.

Each day I become more gifted at recognizing joy.

Tethering Our Hearts to God

. . . .

RELATIONSHIPS ARE THE THREADS WITH which God weaves our earthly world. The ways we relate to and care for each other create the pattern from which our society is fashioned. When relationship strands are weak, the very fabric of life becomes frayed. Therefore, if we're to have the cohesive, creative, and peaceful existence for which we yearn, we need to strengthen and deepen our close relationship ties with God, ourselves, and others.

Our ability to love others unconditionally grows out of our ability to open our hearts to both ourselves and to God. When we tether our hearts to the heart of the Beloved, our relationships become threads worthy of the loom of God.

The following meditation has been helpful for my clients and myself when we seem to be disconnected from God and are floating untethered in a vast and shadowy void.

Gently close your eyes and place your hands over your heart. Concentrate on breathing deeply and evenly while allowing tension to melt and flow away from your body. If your mind wanders, simply return your focus to your breath. Aloud, either say or sing, "Mother/Father God (or use a name with which you resonate), please show me anything that separates me from thee." Utter this prayer from deep within the core of your heart, truly yearning for the answer. Open yourself to insights, awarenesses, or symbols, then ask your wise heart and guardian angels to help you heal and bless whatever appears to be separating you from God.

In the perfect, right way for you, visualize an exquisite cord emanating from your heart into the heart of the Beloved. Feel the energy of unconditional love flowing between you. From your sanctified and overflowing heart, send out a rush of gratitude to those you love, to God, and to all of Her creations.

I am eternally and joyfully connected to God.

My life is woven from threads of love.

Sending Appreciation

. . . .

WE'VE ALL HEARD ABOUT POURING OIL ON troubled waters, and, when we generously pour the oil of appreciation onto our lives and loves, there will be fewer troubled waters for us to wade through. The oil of appreciation energizes all it touches, for appreciation comes from the heart, which is the throne of the Spirit.

One of the best ways to build our appreciation muscles is to bless everything and everyone, especially our family and friends. Without the oil of appreciation, our relationships with family and friends can become dry and chafing.

When Sonya first came to see me, she was puzzled about why it was difficult for her to be around her father. He was a nice, respectable man and a good father, but she felt inadequate and uncomfortable in his presence. Eventually it dawned on Sonya that her dad never said anything complimentary to her. Although he was polite and mouthed "thank-yous," he never highlighted any personal positives of Sonya's. In therapy, Sonya realized how much she longed to be told by her dad what, if anything, he appreciated about her and her accomplishments. Although she could not change who he was, she did learn from the experience to shower others with her appreciation.

To practice sending appreciation, center your awareness in your heart and rest there for a few minutes with no expectations, just breathe in and out. In your mind's eye allow yourself to go to a beautiful place. Glancing around, appreciate the beauty and charm of the place you have chosen. After a minute, very gently begin to appreciate yourself, both for who you are and for your willingness to learn and grow. Invite family members and friends to join you in this meditation. Send appreciation to each one. For a difficult person, find at least one characteristic or one tiny action that you can appreciate. If the waters between you are very troubled, you may only be able to appreciate how many times they have given you the opportunity to practice patience.

By sending silent strands of appreciation we bless others and strengthen the bonds between us and them and between ourselves and our spirits.

I find something to appreciate about everyone.
I deserve to be blessed by appreciation from others.

Being Thankful for Aging

. . . .

IF OLD AGE IS THE VERDICT OF LIFE, gratitude softens the verdict. Overturning the youth-is-panacea verdict pronounced by our society is a crucial spiritual requirement of our time, one that will enable us to reap the fruits of wisdom from each season.

The feminine Spirit deeply understands the natural cycles of life and welcomes them with reverence. In reuniting with our own innate spiritual wisdom we, too, will gracefully journey through the seasons until we grow into the simple elegance of winter and soar to the benevolent mystery of death.

It's early autumn as I write this; ripe fruits and vegetables beckon from roadside stands and trees shyly announce their intention to sleep. I love this time of year. Perhaps it's because I am an early autumn age, but there's something else—a promise of glory—awesome, breathtaking foliage made even more poignant by its being a prelude to the stark, bare branches of winter that have an elegant and uncomplicated beauty of their own. It is a cycle we trust. Spring will follow winter.

Author May Sarton, expressed the beauty of aging when she said in her later years: "Old age is not an illness, it is a timeless ascent. As power diminishes, we grow more toward the light." And, isn't *that* power—to grow toward and be closer to the all-loving Light?

Sit quietly for a moment, breathe deeply, and draw into your body and soul a sense of peaceful gratitude. Allow your mind to float back over the ages you have grown through and, with gratitude, bless them for the joy experienced, the sorrow weathered, and the wisdom gathered. Now invite a picture or sense of who you will be at older ages to come into your mind's eye. Bless this woman as she bridges age to age. Encourage her to flower into the unique and beautiful bloom she is meant to be. Tap into her native strength as she begins to wilt physically. Treasure her essence, which is an eternal fragrance.

I am thankful for each day that I am blessed to live upon Mother Earth.

I reap the harvest of wisdom from each season of my life.

Subsidizing Our Spirit by
Paying Bills with Thanks

· ·

ONE OF THE BEST WAYS TO DRINK FROM THE
wellspring of Spirit is to adopt the attitude: *All
that I do is spiritual.* Being waylaid by spiritually
depleting beliefs in lack and meaninglessness is
enervating and leads to feelings of discourage-
ment. On the other hand, realizing that everything we do can be seen as spiritual and acting
as such bolsters our spirits with enthusiasm and
a sense of purpose.

We can go to the wellspring of Spirit with a
Dixie cup punched full of holes by worry, resentment, or a half-empty mentality, or we can
lift a chalice to the Source that is lined with a
water-tight belief in the sacredness of all things.

For Janice, a successful real estate broker,
her hole-punching nemesis was writing the
monthly alimony check to her former husband.
As the first of the month approached, her jaws
began to tighten and by the time she wrote the
actual check she was a resentment-ridden mess.
After a concerned friend asked her, "Who is this
hurting?" Janice began to wonder how she
could bypass the pain of paying that loathsome

bill. For the first two months, she had the money automatically deducted from her account, but she still obsessed about it, "He probably got the money today, the jerk!" Who was still being hurt? Punch, punch, drip, drip, leak, leak.

Knowing that gratitude could lift her spirits, Janice finally decided to pretend to write "Thank you" on the memo line of the alimony check. "Thank you for being out of my life"; "Thank you for my lessons in what kind of man *not* to choose" were two of her first unwritten acknowledgements. But a funny thing happened. Eventually, she really did feel thankful, and sending off the check became a ritual of appreciation for all that she had learned from the relationship. She was free.

Through each everyday experience we can draw from the infinite well of Spirit. What size cup will you take to the well today?

All that I do is sacred.
I pay bills with a "Thank-you."

Dining with Detractors

PEOPLE WHO ARE THE BIGGEST DETRACTORS in our lives are often also our most valuable teachers. Out of the wounds inflicted by these severe critics, harsh teachers, and wielders of heavy and harmful blows can come much of our compassion and the majority of our strength. Without question, given a preview of coming detractions, we probably wouldn't have invited such folks, or the resultant pain, into our lives. Nonetheless, we are indebted to them for the heart-growing, soul-tempering wisdom derived from our relationship with them.

Gracing these severe teachers with the blessing of gratitude frees us, and them, to move onto softer and sweeter experiences. A wonderful way to say good-bye and sever the connection spiritually is to invite our detractors to dinner, in meditation. Before the event takes place, make careful preparations. First and foremost, decide how you will protect yourself while sharing psychic space with these people. Then compile your guest list; who will be seated where and by whom? What will be served? How will the table look?

When the preparations are finished, invite them to enter and take their seats. Observe these persons who have caused you pain, and carefully make an inventory of the gifts that they (no doubt, inadvertently) have given you in terms of soul growth and personality polishing. Thank each one of them for their contribution to your evolution. If you can't actually feel gratitude, ask the Beloved to open your heart so that gratitude toward them can seep into your soul.

Believe me, I am personally aware that this is not an easy dinner to hostess. Although I do feel thankful for lessons learned from her, I've not yet been able to invite one of my family members to share my psychic table. But I intend to do so one day for she taught me much, and I don't want to drag her energy with me throughout eternity.

Thankfulness helps heal our scars from the inside out and unveil the gifts of wisdom and compassion gleaned from receiving them.

I give thanks for my teachers.

I am stronger in the places where I've been wounded.

Embracing Angels
and
Other Emissaries

*For he shall give his angels charge
over you, to keep you in all your ways.
They shall bear you up in their hands,
lest you dash your foot against a stone.*

Psalms 91:11–12

OUR SPIRIT WANTS TO SURRENDER TO that which it perceives as higher and holier than itself. We need noble role models, and God is hard to visualize. To resolve this dilemma, and yet not singe our circuits to a frazzle with Her overwhelming power and majesty, I think the Beloved encourages angels and other emissaries to intercede on Her behalf. A widely held belief affirms that at least two angels are entrusted with our care at birth, and that others, including the Archangels themselves, are happy to assist us when we call upon them.

I have never seen an angelic being with my physical eyes, but I know several very down-to-earth people who have. On several occasions, however, I have been lovingly protected and guided by invisible, but obviously present, forces. I like to think that these forces were angels, celestial beings of some kind, or energy from my own higher Self. Given my experiences, and others I've heard about, I can't help but believe that just outside of our range of perception we are encircled by angels or guides, the spirits of those whom we have loved and lost, and emissaries from our personal soulselves. And with that certainty comes incredible peace of mind.

Waiting in the Wings

. . . .

YES, ALL THE WORLD'S A STAGE AND ALL THE men and women merely players, as Shakespeare said, but we are also the writers, producers, and directors of our life's play. Luckily, angels wait in the wings to be our prompters, guides, companions, and healers.

Running late, Maggie sprinted through the halls of the hospital, thinking only about where she would get gas for her car's empty tank after she finished visiting this patient. Imagine her amazement when she dashed through the door of the woman's room and saw an angel bending over the sleeping figure. The angel looked up, also surprised, smiled, and vanished. A child of the sixties, Maggie said, "Whoa! I've never experienced such a rush out of *anything* like I did out of seeing that angel!"

Not as dramatic, but nonetheless welcome, was an encounter I had one inky night alone in my car. Coming home from a pottery class, I decided to take an out-in-the-boonies shortcut that I'd only used previously during the day. Presumably, to forestall such shortcuts, someone had barricaded the little road and I was forced to turn around. When I backed up, my car fell in a hole and I was "turtled" helplessly on a hump, wheels in a hole and undercarriage caught on who knew what. It was pitch black and quite a long way from home.

Panicking, I called out to my mother who had been dead for several years. "Mother, it's Sue and my car and I are in trouble! Please help me! . . ." Daring to hope, I gunned the motor again, the car popped out of the hole and I made it home safely. Gene and I went back to check the hole the next day. My tire tracks were there and he said, "Only a miracle got you out of that hole." Yes, one performed by an angel waiting in the wings.

Today, cheer and comfort yourself by knowing that, just behind the curtain, your angels wait to help enhance your life's play.

I have angels waiting in the wings.
It's perfectly okay to ask for help.

Opening the Windows

. . . .

"GOD, WHOSE LOVE AND JOY ARE PRESENT everywhere, can't come to visit you unless you art there!" I love that wise adage from Meister Eckhart; it so succinctly states the obvious. By throwing open the windows of our souls through awareness and quiet contemplation, we will be able to welcome God's calling cards of light, love, joy, and solace.

Although daylight will peep through a very small hole, how much better to fling the windows of our souls wide in welcome to angels and other emissaries who come bearing gifts. The Beloved has a keen sense of humor and drama, and celestial callers can appear quite unexpectedly. We have to be on the lookout.

Diane felt restless and lonely one sunny day several months after the death of her mother and decided to take a drive. Admittedly feeling sorry for herself, she was lamenting how much she wished she could see her mother and know that she was all right. Suddenly, swooping in front of the car, sun gleaming on its white head, came an eagle (often said by native peoples to be messengers from the Great Spirit). Diane stopped the car and watched the eagle settle in the top of a tree. As she whispered, "Mom, is that you?" the eagle swiveled its head disdainfully and looked down as if to say, "Of course not! But she did send me." Diane laughed and felt her heart lift.

Tom, a conservative older gentleman, hesitantly revealed to me that his wife had appeared to him as her casket was being lowered into the ground. "I must have imagined it!" he said, "But the funny thing is, when she smiled at me, I got the feeling that I just might be able to make it through this."

Believed in or doubted, anticipated or unexpected, angels and other emissaries will fly through the open windows of our souls, lifting our hearts in the process.

Angels love me and look out for me.

I open the windows of my soul to welcome light and love.

Finding Peace in Silence and Solitude

. . . .

THE OVERSTIMULATION OF TOO MUCH BUSY-ness chafes our souls and makes it impossible for us to recognize any angels gracing our lives. If we're constantly rubbing shoulders with others, rarely alone, seldom awash in silence but often engulfed by outside demands, we can become irritated and afflicted with what I call diaper rash of the soul. Red, raw, and ugly low-grade pain, usually hidden from view.

Itchy and irritated feelings are clues that we need to close the door on chaos and take time to rest, replenish, and restore our own souls. For most of us, it's in the quiet company of our selves that we are most likely to be soothed by the peaceful caress of caring angels. Metaphorically fanned by the soft wings of silence and solitude, we can cool our frenzy, quiet our minds, and mellow our attitudes. In silence, it's possible to drink deeply from the pure well of peace waiting at the center of our souls.

White Eagle, a wonderful Native American teacher, has this to say about finding peace, "You long for peace. You think of peace as being goodwill among the nations, the laying down of arms. But peace is far more than this, it can only be understood and realized within your heart. It lies beneath all the turmoil and noise and clamor of the world, beneath feeling, beneath thought. It is found in the deep, deep silence and stillness of the soul. It is spirit; it is God."

Find a place and time when you can arrange for silence and solitude. For some of us, the best we can do is a few extra minutes locked in the bathroom. That's okay. Close your eyes and softly sigh into the silence. If there is background noise, listen to the silence between sounds. Concentrate on your heart, and follow a welcoming pathway deep into it. The path ends at a beautiful well. Rest there. Replenish. In peace-filled solitude, drink in the stillness of your soul.

Peace is the Goddess softly whispering to our souls.

I give myself permission to close the door on chaos.

I rest and replenish with silence and solitude.

Expecting Holiness from God Alone

· ·

It is not because angels are holier than men
or devils that makes them angels, but because
they do not expect holiness from another,
but from God alone.

—William Blake

ISN'T THE ABOVE STATEMENT A PERFECT ONE
for those of us who tend to be perfectionists?
According to Blake, we can don angelic robes
simply by giving up our expectations of perfect
holiness from ourselves! Merely surrendering
into the reality that we are flawed, imperfect,
and yet marvelously miraculous humans will
actually advance us a rung or two up Jacob's
ladder.

Being a recovering perfectionist, I find
Blake's idea very appealing. Each time I'm more
gentle with myself and others, can I tuck a little
white feather into my symbolic wings? If I give
up perfection as a prerequisite for worthiness
and being lovable, will it put some spit and polish on my halo? Can learning to laugh good-

humoredly at my foibles help me fly a little higher? Probably so.

Let's try it right now and see. Allow your eyes to close gently and your breath to deepen. As you inhale, draw in a sense of acceptance for yourself exactly as you are now. As you exhale, release any judgments and criticisms of yourself and ask your angels to transform the energy of perfectionism into the ideal energy for your soul's evolution. Without being critical of yourself, think of a time when your quest for perfection made you or someone else unhappy or uncomfortable. As if you had already given up expecting perfection and holiness from yourself, replay the encounter in precisely the way you would have liked it to be. Imagine yourself in a celestial costume shop and, for every step away from perfectionism you took in the replay, clothe yourself in a piece of angel raiment.

God's job description includes holy perfection; ours does not.

I accept and love myself as I am.
I accept and love others as they are.

Reflecting the Face of God

. . . .

AS WOMEN OF SPIRIT, WE ARE GIVEN THE opportunity to reflect the face of God to those whom we love and to those whose lives we breeze through briefly. What does the face of God reflect? Of course, we're not altogether certain, but let's assume that God is love far beyond our ability to envision. In that case, Her face would surely reflect unconditional love, a wish to bless all of her children, a longing to bring solace to those seared by pain, an acceptance of the bumblings and stumblings natural to emotional and spiritual growth, and a desire to encourage and support creative efforts.

Most of us are already gifted at reflecting the face of God. And we can become even dearer blessings by more closely following the urgings of our hearts which are, in essence, reflections of the Divine.

All morning, the image of a woman whom Molly only slightly knew kept popping into her mind. Because she had been touched by reading portions of the woman's latest book, she dismissed the urge to call, thinking that her mind was just ruminating on the ideas in the book. Unable to shake the urge to call the author,

Molly asked her heart for guidance. "Call!" came the immediate message. When Molly phoned and thanked the writer for the beauty of the book and for the hope that it had instilled in her, the woman burst into tears. It turned out that the author was having one of those down-in-the-dumps, doubting days when she wondered if her work was worth the effort and if anyone really benefited from it. She sorely needed encouragement. By listening to the wise angel-urgings of her heart, Molly became a blessing to the author and, in doing so, reflected the face of God.

Acting from our hearts brushes us all with the gentle wings of love. What loving act can you make today?

I listen and act on the urgings of my heart.

To the best of my ability,
I reflect the face of God to others.

Asking for Guidance

. . . .

AROUND US, AND WITHIN OUR HEARTS AND souls, resides a plethora of helpers willing to pour forth a wealth of insight. At any time we can ask for inspiration, instruction, and understanding, and angels and other emissaries will respond. Granted, their answers are often subtle and devilishly hard to decipher. To help us trust in the authenticity of angelic help and the reality of receiving inspiration and instruction, prayers and meditations like the following are invaluable.

Tamilou, a spiritually dedicated young woman, uses this beautiful prayer when feeling the need for special guidance. To prepare, Tamilou randomly selects an Angel Card and casts a circle of light around herself. Then she prays, "Dear Goddess, please give me divine knowledge, divine wisdom, and divine guidance. Give me the truth, not my wishful thinking or my worst fears." Having asked for what she wants, Tamilou becomes receptive by silently meditating or writing in her journal. While the answers she seeks are only rarely immediate or obvious, they do appear eventually.

A meditation that I find both helpful and soul-lifting is to envision meeting a person, or persons, with whom I resonate spiritually. For me, such a beloved wisdom teacher might be Christ (or Jeshua, as his family called him), a Being named The Lady, or the Mother Mary as the strong, wise, and gentle woman I have come to believe that she was and is.

If you can, turn within now. Magnetize your energy back to your own body, heart, and spirit from all of the places it has been dispersed today. Think of a spiritual being with whom you resonate. Meet them in a beautiful place that is comfortable for you both and be with them in the ways that feel right for you now. You may want guidance or you may need solace and comfort. Ask for what you want and need.

Angels and other emissaries want to serve us. Our challenge is to believe and ask.

Beloved and blessed wisdom teachers please guide me.

I believe my prayers are answered.

Invoking Archangels

. . . .

I WANT TO SHARE A WONDERFUL PRAYER invoking the four archangels, which is adapted from an ancient, mystical Jewish prayer. In it, we call in the archangels Uriel, Michael, Raphael, and Gabriel to encircle us with their presence. Please feel free to personalize it to suit yourself.

First, I invoke the angel Uriel in front of me, focus on that area and try to feel his loving presence. Uriel is the angel of clarity and discrimination, and I pray something like this, "Uriel, please clear my mind. Help me have clarity of vision, purity of heart, and wise discrimination." If I'm confused about a particular issue, I'll ask for clarity with it.

Then, on my right side, I call for Michael, who is the angel of love and loving kindness. I always like to bask in his presence for a few minutes before asking, "Michael, please show me how to open my heart in true loving kindness, especially when I feel fundamentally unloving. Help me graciously accept your love and the love of others, and guide me in the right way to love myself, others, and the world. Flow through me, please."

On my left side, I invoke the angel Gabriel, who brings strength and helps overcome fear. If I have a special fear or need, I pray about it. If not, I just ask for strength in general.

Behind me is Raphael, the angel of healing. I ask him to care for any of my specific ills or concerns, and then I invite him to care for the healing needs of others. I also invite him to move into my body, permeating all of my being with his healing energy.

After invoking the four archangels, I ask that their love flow into my heart and then out to others who are in need of help and blessing. During the day, I try to remember their nearness and feel their closeness.

Archangels Uriel, Michael, Gabriel, and Raphael love to answer when I call.

I am encircled by angelic love.

Blessings from Cherubs

· ·

POLLY ARRIVED AT HER SON'S PRESCHOOL A little early, so she sat down with him and his friends at the snack table. Three-year-old Jeremiah, who is so adorable that he could be an artist's model posing for cherubs, put his arm around his mother, looked up at her, and said, "I was in heaven with God and he gave me a choice of moms, and I chose you!"

Any mother would be thrilled with such a statement, but it was a heart-lifting blessing for Polly because at that moment she was in the throes of struggling with chronic depression and low self-esteem and felt as if she could hardly drag herself through the day. Her son's comment brightened the gathering darkness. In his own angelic way, Jeremiah had assured his mom that she was a beautiful being, worthy of love. Indeed, *chosen* for love.

Whenever you get the chance, gather a blessing from a cherub. If you do not have children of your own, chortle at a baby in the grocery store and let her smile light up your day. Wave to children as they play. Find a painting or card of a darling baby and put it where his innocence can twinkle at you.

If there are no little ones, fresh from God, in your life, you can invite their presence through creative imagination. Softly close your eyes and allow your breath to deepen. Let your imagination soar into a realm where the Beloved Mother is playing with a number of babies. Be content to merely observe the scene until you feel especially drawn to one or two of the cherubs and then, in a way that feels comfortable to you, join them. Absorb the blessing of their joyous purity, and be cheered by their delight in you.

As a new grandmother, I've come to believe that being anointed by the blessing of cherubs is experiencing a love similar to the pure, unconditional love with which the Beloved holds us.

There is within me a pure and joyous cherub.

The Beloved loves me unconditionally.

Catching God's Drift

. . . .

SPIRIT IS ALWAYS COMMUNICATING WITH US via intuition, but regularly we don't catch the drift. Maybe we're deafened by the roar of demands from family and work or too busy elsewhere to interpret symbols when they appear, feel the soft breeze of God's loving caress, or hear the silent insights whispered in our ears by angels. As Antoine de Saint-Exupery explained in *The Little Prince,* "It is only with the heart that one can see rightly; what is essential is invisible to the eye." Therefore, it is by making space for ourselves and opening our hearts in awareness that we more easily catch God's drift.

Animals are favorite emissaries of spiritual messages. One morning I was walking by a stream, concentrating on opening my heart by singing the chant, "Lord, please let me see anything that stands between me and thee." I rounded a corner and saw two wolves looking down at me from a wildlife-rescue facility across the water. The largest wolf was white and the smaller, black. Touched, my knees started shaking.

Seeing the wolves was especially moving to me because I have had recurring dreams in which a white and a black wolf play the central parts. To me they are guardians of my well-being, symbols of masculine and feminine divine energy. Staring at these magnificent beings, I felt seen and cared for by the Spirit within me and the unfathomable mystery surrounding me. The message I caught was, "I hear you. I am as close as breath and as far as your disregard and distraction."

Today, please give yourself the essential gifts of an open heart and quiet time alone in nature—a small corner of a garden or loving and appreciating a house plant; even looking at the moon and stars through the window is fine if you are housebound or live in the city. We catch the drift of heavenly communion in the sacred center of our open hearts.

Lord, please help me see anything
that comes between me and thee.

God is as close as my breath.

Creating and Accepting Sanctuary

. . . .

The very seams of my soul
Feel frayed by the weight of
           death
               business
                  loneliness

I long to collapse in
        angels' arms
And let them gently knit me
Back together

I WROTE THE ABOVE POEM WHILE LONGING
for a sanctuary of solace and support. We all go
through times when we need a metaphorical—
and sometimes actual—lap to crawl into and lay
down our weary heads. For emotional and spiritual health, we require friends whom we can
count on to provide strength when we are vulnerable, comfort when we are aching, and guidance when we are confused. We all need
spiritual sisters whose wings are powerful
enough for two when ours are limp and useless.
More than likely you provide a lap and wings

for others, but do you have angel's arms in which to collapse if need be?

If the answer is yes, wonderful. If it is no, it is possible *and* essential to create such support.

Desiree was worn out by countless family demands and badly needed a friend to bounce her feelings off of. It was late and she didn't want to disturb me by calling, so in her imagination she invited me to sit across from her for tea and conversation. "I" just listened at first, Desiree said, and then gave her some good suggestions about how to take care of herself. Although she knew that I wasn't there in person, she felt much better after our "conversation."

What a great lesson for all of us! If friends are physically unavailable, we can conjure up an *internal* soul-sister or angel and allow her to be our sanctuary. The important thing is that we encourage ourselves to create sanctuaries in which to heal, rest, and replenish. The soul of spiritual friendship, like the sole of a shoe, allows us to walk on rocks with less pain.

I love myself enough to ask for support.
I provide a lap and wings for myself and others

Entering the Harbor of Hope

· ·

HOPE IS AN ANGELIC ATTITUDE. IT HELPS US see silver linings hidden within dark clouds and rise above trial, tribulation, and disappointment. Without hope, our spiritual light is doomed to be very dim, as Dante suggested in the *Inferno* when he wrote that the sign over the entrance to Hell read, "Abandon hope all ye who enter here."

Hope is a safe harbor in which we can find refuge when the storms of life roughly toss us around or the flotsam and jetsam of frustration batters our hulls. I have had times in my life when I felt so engulfed by misery that I didn't know if I could keep my nose above water one more day. At one point, if it hadn't been for my children, I may not have had the courage to stay in the fray. Like sand in an hour glass, hope had drained from my spirit. Luckily, I had life-jackets other than my children, and they held me up until I could tread a little water under my own power. As I regained strength, the following meditation helped reinforce my spiritual ballast.

Gently close your eyes and focus on your breath, allowing it to float effortlessly in and out. With each inhalation, imagine that you are drawing the energy of hope into your body and soul. It doesn't matter if you feel hopeful, the intention toward hopefulness is enough for now. Briefly, think of any circumstance, feeling, or belief that is creating stormy seas for you. Notice that a short distance away is a quiet, serene, and welcoming harbor. Angels, friends, or other emissaries beckon for you to come into the harbor and, intuitively, you know that increased serenity and calm waits for you there. As you enter the harbor of hope, you are greeted by Beings who will care for you compassionately. Rest with them and allow them to minister to you.

Anointed with the angelic attitude of hope, raging seas are calmed and balance and harmony is restored.

I am a woman filled with hope.

I turn to friends and angels for infusions of hope.

Becoming the Arms of God

. . . .

WE ARE GOD AND GODDESS' ARMS PRESENT in the world. Who needs a hug? Who needs a heart-lift? Whose groceries need to be bought? Who needs a willing ear to listen to their story? Whose rights need to be championed? Who needs a hand to hold? When we offer our arms (or hearts and ears) for these services, we are offering a tangible fragment of God's love to one of her children. We will, as the hymn says, be like "angels descending, bring from above, echoes of mercy, whispers of love."

Each morning, before getting out of bed, Brenda breathes a request to the Divine. "Beloved Friend, I open myself to be of service. Please help me be your arms and willingly hold those who need a healing touch. Open my eyes that I may see what you ask of me today. Open my ears that I may truly hear and respond to the cries of joy and sorrow from your children. May the words of my mouth be the meditations of your heart, and may I sow peace wherever I go. Thank you."

Expressing and acting out our soul's angelic energy—becoming a circle of love for ourselves and others—is one of our highest callings. In living a life of spirit, we are challenged to surrender to the highest and holiest within us and become an advocate, a guardian angel of protection and strength, and a comforter for our dear friend, self, and for those whose lives we touch. Although we may question our ability to undertake such a mission, we are qualified for the assignment because each of us is, herself, a daughter of the Divine. With hearts, arms, eyes, and ears open we will know how the Divine yearns to love through us.

I am yours, Beloved, use me as an angel of love.
My heart and arms are open to myself and others.

Unfurling Our Wings

. . . .

I'VE HEARD IT SAID THAT THE POWER WITHIN us doesn't wake up until *we* do. What does waking up mean? I believe waking up means that we women, individually and collectively, need to accept the reality that, when our wings are unfurled, we are powerful spiritual beings with a huge capacity for bringing healing to ourselves, one another, and our planet. A woman's wings naturally contain the nurturing feathers of inclusion, cooperation, acceptance, compassion, wisdom, intuition, and love—all qualities that our society needs in large measure.

If our own wings have been clipped by disrespect, dishonor, lack of opportunity, or mistreatment—and most women's have to a greater or lessor degree—then our first priority is to heal ourselves. To become an angel, we must, first, allow ourselves to heal in the embrace of angels.

Visualize yourself standing in a beautiful ray of sunshine. Before you is a full-length mirror in which you see yourself reflected wearing your spiritual wings. Examine them carefully. Can they freely and easily unfurl? If not, what do they need in order to soar as they were made to do? If you don't like the way they look or feel, change them. You are the artist; create wings that please you. Don't hesitate to ask for assistance in refurbishing your wings if you would like it. Practice unfurling your fabulous wings and, like a mother dove, spread them protectively over others.

Fortunately, we have guides along our spiritual paths who help us heal and are continually issuing wake-up calls that encourage us to unfurl our wings, empower ourselves, and live in harmony with our unique truth. Insights, flashes of intuition, and hunches are all nudges from inner or outer angels, urging us to wake up to and live from our unique wisdom. As we do, healing will take place.

Protecting ourselves and all of our Mother's children under the wings of love is our awesome mission, and we can accomplish it by simply being our true selves.

I fly on wings of love.
I am a powerful spiritual being.

Bearing the Light

· ·

WHILE WE ARE CONTINUALLY SURROUNDED by the support and love of angels, we are also called upon to be Emissaries of the Light and intermediaries for the Divine in some situations. As White Eagle tells us, "You are a bearer of the Light, for you are as the Divine Mother, bearing within you the Light of the Son. Take the Light out into the world to bless and to heal, and quicken the vibrations of the whole earth." Our calls, which often come in the form of intuitive nudges and emotional hits, probably mean that someone is in need of our intercession and help.

One early morning, I awoke suddenly at 4:45 A.M. with a foreboding feeling about my son. I've learned to pay attention to those intuitive prods and, knowing that he was taking part in the Baltimore Triathlon that day, surrounded him with light and prayed, "Mother/Father God, I ask that any negative circumstance that may befall Brett will be transformed and transmuted through love into the perfect, right experience," until I finally fell back to sleep around 7:30.

Sure enough, one of Brett's tires blew out during the bike race, but, although he was in the middle of the pack, all of the other riders managed to avoid him. No one was hurt, thank God. It was very disappointing for him to go all that way and be disqualified, but it could have been much worse.

When you feel the urge to pray for someone, you can breathe them into your heart and then out into the care of their angels, or use the prayer I prayed for Brett, or repeat the Protection Prayer, which is: "The light of God surrounds you, the love of God enfolds you, the power of God protects you, and the presence of God watches over you. Wherever you are, God is," or whatever your wisdom guides you to do.

We bear the white light and ability to pray, which have the power to mitigate if not change circumstances.

I bear the light of the Divine Mother.

I listen to my intuitive nudges and act on them.

Acknowledgments

. . . .

I AM ACUTELY AWARE THAT THERE IS NO WAY to thank everyone who has blessed my life and supported my passion for writing, so I would just like to say at the outset, if you have touched my life, however briefly or lightly, I am deeply appreciative. Without your influence, I would have missed sprinkles of fairy-dust, grains of wisdom, drops of growth, and lots of laughs.

As ever, a resounding thank you to my wonderful husband, Gene, for everything he does and is, but especially for his encouragement, humor, and hugs. I feel deep gratitude for all of the special people at Conari Press who bring the spirit of love and integrity into the office. Kudos to Ame for her talent and unending patience and to Brenda for her creativity and mystical spirit. Mary Jane, a thousand thank yous for being a gifted editor and a treasured friend. Teary eyed thank yous to Josh, our first grandchild, for gracing our family with his irresistible smile and angelic, impish self, and to Lynnie and Shawn who gave him life. Mike, Brett, and Paige, thank you for being not only our children but our friends and teachers as well.

Annabelle, Bonnie, Judith, Sherrie, Ruth, Mickey, Patti, Susan, Paula, Cece, Phyllis, Betty, Connie, Carolyn, Chris, Muriel, Gayle, Sarge, Jo, Karen, and Juli, thank you for your circles of love and prayers. To Franci and Kathlyn and all of the teachers whose lives and works have been an inspiration to me, my appreciation.

May blessings rain upon each of you named here or held silently within the core of my heart.

Personal Note

. . . .

I hope that you experience as much joy and heart-opening from reading *The Woman's Book of Spirit* as I have from writing it. To share a small part of my spiritual journey with soul-sisters has been a particular joy. If you would like to share some of your journey with me, I would love to hear it from you.

To tell me of your spiritual quest, or to purchase autographed copies of any of my books, please write to me:

Sue Patton Thoele
P.O. Box 1519
Boulder, CO 80306-1519

Sue Patton Thoele

Licensed psychotherapist Sue Patton Thoele is the author of THE COURAGE TO BE YOURSELF, THE WOMAN'S BOOK OF CONFIDENCE, THE WOMAN'S BOOK OF COURAGE, THE WOMAN'S BOOK OF SPIRIT, AUTUMN OF THE SPRING CHICKEN, and HEART CENTERED MARRIAGE. She and her husband, Gene, live in Boulder, Colorado, and have four adult children, a son-in-law, and one grandson.